Emptiness and Bliss

Mastering Energy and Consciousness on the Journey Towards Enlightenment

To Tomoko & Darrell,

I hope you will enjoy this book and get inspired to shine your light even brighter.

With Love,

Stef xx

STEF KLING

Copyright © 2016 Stef Kling

All rights reserved. No part of this book may be used or reproduced in any form without written permission of the author, except in the case of brief quotations used in critical articles and reviews.

ISBN: 1540315789
ISBN-13: 978-1540315786

CREDITS

Cover design by Prodesignsx

Photograph of J. Krishnamurti by Edward Weston
Quotes from J. Krishnamurti (chapter 5) reproduced with permission. Permission to quote from the works of J. Krishnamurti or other works for which the copyright is held by the Krishnamurti Foundation of America or the Krishnamurti Foundation Trust Ltd has been given on the understanding that such permission does not indicate endorsement of the views expressed in this publication. For more information about J. Krishnamurti please see: www.jkrishnamurti.org

The seven levels of consciousness (chapter 33) are based on the model from *"Handbook to Higher Consciousness"* by Ken Keyes, jr.

All other known sources have been listed in the text. Rights holders of any copyrighted works not credited should contact the Author for a correction to be made in the next edition or reprinting of this book.

For Vicky

Several people have given me support and inspiration in various ways during this project: Leona Kling, Ben Drake, Jan Sandor, Fleur Barnfather and Lucy Thom, to name a few. Several clients have been so kind to give me permission to use their cases as examples in this book. You know who you are. Karolina Mikulicz held the space beautifully for me in the rebirthing session in which I entered into the second wave of awakening. But especially I want to thank Rachel Harford for her proof reading and enthusiastic encouragement, and Ruth O'Neil for her superb and patient editing skills. I love you.

Contents

About the Author — 6
Introduction — 7

Part One: The energetics of enlightenment
1. My awakening experience — 11
2. Making sense of it — 19
3. What is enlightenment? — 21
4. Yogananda (1893 – 1952) — 23
5. Krishnamurti (1895 – 1986) — 28
6. Osho (1931 – 1989) — 33
7. Papaji (1910 – 1997) — 39
8. Andrew Cohen — 46
9. Mooji — 49
10. Adyashanti — 52
11. Eckhart Tolle — 55
12. Understanding enlightenment — 59

Part Two: The 5 principles of spiritual growth
13. The 5 principles of spiritual growth — 73
14. Stages of spiritual development — 75
15. Releasing your emotion — 87
16. Raising your frequency — 91
17. Healing your ego — 103
18. Raising your consciousness — 106
19. Connecting to source — 109

Part Three: Releasing your emotions
20. It's all about emotions — 119
21. How stress kills your body — 122
22. Storing emotions — 125
23. Your emotions rule your mind — 130
24. Your emotions create your life — 133
25. Releasing emotions — 138
26. Recapitulation — 143
27. Ho'oponopono — 147

28. The Emotion Code	154
29. Some personal experiences	162
30. Conclusion	165

Part Four: Raising your consciousness

31. Introduction	169
32. Seven levels of consciousness	170
33. Your mind is a filter	173
34. The power of beliefs	176
35. Your imagination is real	178
36. Your story	180
37. You create your own reality	184
38. You always have a choice	186
39. Intention or Inspiration	189
40. Fate and Destiny	192
41. Karma	195
42. Your mind is a beast	198
43. Luxury problems	200
44. Acceptance	205
45. Forgiveness	208
46. Gratitude	211
47. We know nothing	213
48. Fear	216
49. Love	219
50. Love or Fear	223
51. The illusion of happiness	226
52. Letting go	229
53. Death	231
54. Nothing matters	234
55. Who am I?	237
56. Why am I here?	241
57. You are already enlightened	244
58. Life without limits	246
59. Total freedom	247
60. Permanent peace	249
Epilogue	251

About the Author

Stef Kling was born in 1968 in Holland. From a young age he felt that he did not come here to have a "normal" life: a steady job, a house, a wife and two kids. As a teenager, he pursued his dream to compete in the "Whitbread Around The World Yacht Race" – the toughest ocean sailing race there is. But it was not his destiny to become a professional sailor.

In 1996 he started his conscious spiritual journey by learning Reiki (a form of hands-on healing). He spiritually opened up very quickly and in 1997 he learned to communicate with Spirit Guides through the process of Automatic Writing. This is the same process that Neale Donald Walsch used to write his "*Conversations with God*" books. Spirit Guides can be defined as spirits, or souls, who reside on the Astral Plane and mentor and guide us in our life on earth. Over the years, Stef has performed hundreds of readings for other people, writing with their Spirit Guides, gaining invaluable spiritual insights himself in the process.

For a long time, Stef combined his spiritual development with a career in IT Project Management, Human Resources and Interim Management. Eventually, he focussed on working as a Healer and Spiritual Teacher. He uses a wide range of techniques such as: Coaching, Aura Reading, Reiki and The Emotion Code. He gained a thorough grounding in psychology (Psychosynthesis), is drawn to (Zen) Buddhism and the teachings of masters like Osho and Krishnamurti.

It is his mastery of energy and consciousness that opened him to the experiences and insights that are described in this book. He currently lives in England with his daughter Vicky. Stef gives talks and workshops internationally, as well as working individually with clients. See for more info: www.stefkling.com.

Introduction

When I woke up one night in 2014 with a tremendous amount of energy rushing through my whole body, I could not have foreseen the events that would follow over the next two years. It marked the start of the biggest adventure in my life: discovering who I truly am.

This book is a direct consequence of my awakening experience that eventually happened in 2015, and everything that followed. The awakening experience gave me a totally clear insight of what happens energetically when you become enlightened. This is something that hardly ever gets spoken about. It gave me an insight into why a lot of the methods that should lead to enlightenment don't work, at least not for most people.

I discovered that the key is to focus on Emptiness and Bliss, and to combine Energy with Consciousness. I came to understand that there are five main principles that are crucial to reaching enlightenment, but that actually these principles are fundamental for any spiritual growth. They apply to anybody, whether you want to become enlightened or not. If you "just" want to be more happy, have more peace in your life, or want have a better quality of life, these same principles are applicable.

In Part One I will describe my awakening experience, and what it means to be enlightened. To understand this I will discuss some of the most well known enlightened masters of our time: Yogananda, Osho, Krishnamurti, Mooji and Eckhart Tolle, amongst others. It might seem strange to start a book with talking about enlightenment, but if this is the ultimate destination, the ultimate goal, does it not make sense to know a bit more about where we are going in the first place?

In Part Two, I will describe the five principles and give an overview of the whole spiritual journey: from birth to enlightenment and anything in between. Two of these principles are described in more detail in Part Three and Part Four: Releasing your Emotions and Raising your Consciousness.

I hope that this book will give you a better understanding of the spiritual journey, and that the five principles will give you direction on how you can progress further along your path. But knowledge without action is useless, so after you have read the book just try to apply these principles to your life. Play with them, see for yourself if what I am saying is valid or not. If something does not resonate for you, then just drop it. There is no path that is perfect for everybody.

With love,

Stef Kling
December 2016

Part One

The Energetics of Enlightenment

1
My awakening experience

It all started in the spring of 2014. One day in April whilst I was receiving a healing session, I had a vision where I saw a sacred geometric shape stretching out in front of me. I can only describe it as a series of rectangular shapes moving away from me. They were slowly getting smaller, and eventually a bigger and beautiful shining octagonal shape emerged. I recognised this octagonal shape as my personal symbol; the image that symbolises my soul energy. The energy of it was so pure and powerful, it was amazing.
I drew that shape afterwards:

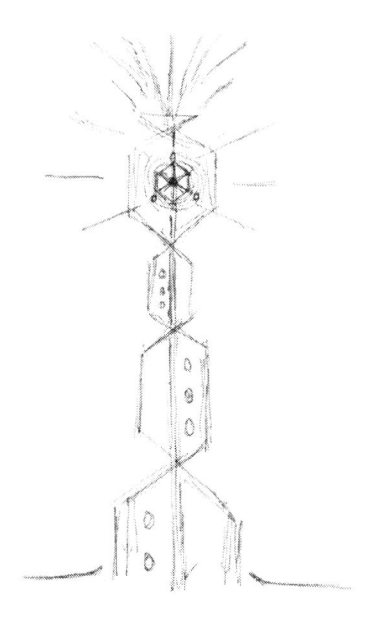

But what did it all mean? When I asked that question I tuned in and I knew somehow that the "rectangles" represented my relationships. I understood that I would have one more relationship, and after that it would end, I would merge with myself and go beyond the need for relationship.

It felt so real, and I started crying. I wanted to have a relationship, in fact I had just fallen in love with someone. I didn't want to be alone, the thought of not having a relationship anymore scared me.

About two weeks later I was sleeping when all of a sudden I woke up in the middle of the night. There were waves of energy running through my body – from my crown down to the tips of my toes. There was so much energy, my whole body was tingling. It was similar to the sensation you have with a very strong Reiki session (*a form of hands on healing*), but then much stronger, running in waves all over my body. I thought: "what is happening?" Then all of a sudden I got the feeling that if I allowed this to continue I would die. Well not literally, but something inside me would die. My ego? I knew that somehow everything would change. But what about Vicky? (*my daughter*) She was sleeping in the room next door, and I needed to look after her (*she lives with me as her mum spends a lot of time abroad*). How would I be able to look after her if I allowed this to happen? With these thoughts fear came in, and I blocked the process. Slowly the energy calmed down. I was boiling - there was so much heat inside me. After some time the energy waves subsided. I managed to calm down, and eventually I fell back to sleep…

After that not much happened for a year.
Fast forward to the spring of 2015. That new relationship didn't work out, and by this time I had met someone else. There was a strong physical attraction, but I was not sure if I really wanted to be with her. She was in love with me, and I spoke openly about my feelings and doubts. In the end we decided to just jump in and see what would happen.

During that time I would strongly feel an energy "hanging above me." It felt like there was like this cloud (or wave) of energy above me, waiting to come in. It was at a yoga festival early in June 2015 that the process started. I could feel an energy coming in through my crown chakra and moving down to my third eye. I could see my octagonal symbol (*as shown in the previous picture*) in my third eye, shining out a red light. Somehow I knew that this was my soul energy. It was so pure, such a high frequency. It was an amazing feeling.

This happened three times during the festival. The third time that it happened, I was so filled with this high energy that when I returned to our tent and my girlfriend wanted to make love, I physically couldn't do it. My frequency was so high that making love felt like a much lower frequency and my body couldn't do it. It was such a weird experience.

After that festival, I somehow knew that I could not be in that relationship anymore. Two weeks later I ended the relationship. At the end of June I went to Glastonbury. Driving on the way back I saw two deer just in front of the car, jumping out of a field on the left, crossing the road and going into the field on the right. I knew that it was symbolic, but I didn't know what it meant at the time. Perhaps something about freedom? About crossing over into new territory?

The next day, it was a Friday (*26 June – 26 is my favourite number*), I woke up and I felt really strange. I had no energy, no drive, didn't want to do anything. I went to the beach, which is my favourite place to be. But even there I didn't feel much, I felt numb. It felt like nothing mattered anymore. Work, relationships… it all didn't matter at all. If I died today it wouldn't matter at all. But what about Vicky? I thought about it, but even that didn't matter. She would live, she would move on. It was the most strange experience, I was observing myself and thought "this is really quite strange." I was worried about what was happening. In the evening I talked to Leona (*my ex-wife who was staying with us for a few weeks*) about it, and said that I was worried about my own mental state. But she said "I'm not worried, it seems that your ego has fallen away, but it will come back." This calmed me down, as I trust her judgment (she is an excellent psychotherapist). So I went to sleep, still in this state.

By now I was operating very slowly. Doing everyday things took me much longer than normal. It was as if my mind slowed down and I stopped feeling. I felt empty, numb, nothingness.

The next morning was a Saturday and we (Leona and I) were driving very early in the morning to London to see Vicky perform at her school's Olympic games. I was still in the same state, feeling empty and numb. At some point we stopped for a coffee. As I drank the coffee I started feeling a bit better, it was as if somehow my energy reconnected with myself. All of a sudden I felt fantastic. I felt SUCH peace! I felt as if all my life I had been seeing through a mist, and now finally the mist had lifted and I could see clearly. For the first time I could really see. But mostly there was this overwhelming feeling of peace. It was as if I had sunk to the bottom of the ocean. All my life so far I have been at the surface, with waves going up and down, sometimes calm but then the next storm would come, more waves would come and I would be going up and down. Now I was at the bottom of the ocean. And at the bottom of the ocean it is calm, there is peace. I was not only at the bottom of the ocean, I was the ocean.

When we arrived in London I didn't want to leave this state, I wanted to stay at the bottom of the ocean, just be with myself. That day I could hardly speak with anyone. I was listening to conversations. It all was such idle chit chat. I was observing and could see everybody completely stuck in their story, in their ego. "Just let me be. I want to sink down to the bottom again." On the journey home I could relax again and return to this state. That evening, whilst I was cleaning up Vicky's tent, I saw two toads. First one, and then a bit later the other. Later that night I saw a post on Facebook that said a toad means transformation. Nice synchronicity.

The next few days I was in and out of this state, but during that week I slowly came back to the surface and started to function a bit better again. I wrote with my guides and asked what happened. They explained that this was the start of a big transformation for me. They said "This was just 40% of the process, the rest will come, probably within the next two weeks." I thought: "Wow, this was only 40%? What will happen next?" But they didn't want to tell me.

By now I had learned that often it is better not to know what will happen. I had a few experiences in the past where I knew what would happen, and sometimes it created a lot of anxiety and stress, other times a lot of excitement. Either way your mind starts to get in the way of the actual experience. In this case I was okay not to know what would happen, and I relaxed.

In the next few days when I meditated on the beach I could feel the energy (subtly) coming in through the crown chakra, this time coming down to my throat chakra, where I felt it got blocked. The red glow had changed into blue. Time passed and in a few days I was going to Holland, so I thought maybe it won't happen.

A friend had offered to do a rebirthing session with me (*a practise where you work with a strong breathing pattern to bring up and transform old stored energies*). I thought it might be interesting to do, and perhaps it could remove the energy block in my throat chakra which was preventing the energy flowing down further.

We talked about my birth, and she asked me if I had any intentions for this session. I somehow knew that I had no birth trauma, but I did want to know (if possible) what my intention was when I decided to come back to earth and be born again. What was my purpose for this life?

I started breathing and somehow I rapidly went back in time during my life. I saw a few things that happened when I was young (my sister, being bullied at school) then I went to my birth – no trauma at all, then I was pre birth and I could feel my purpose: to learn about relationships, and to completely step into my power. My full power. And to bring truth.

Soon after that the energy started to flow in. It came in very strongly through my crown chakra. I knew this was my soul energy. But this was SO STRONG! To help to understand this I can compare it with electricity: if we normally we have 10 Amp electricity running through us, this was 1000 Amp. It was amazing! It was such a great power. And it was such a high frequency! All of a sudden a hot ball of energy ignited at the base of my spine. The incoming energy wave had activated my Kundalini energy. Within a split second it shot up along my spine, and I felt as if I was going to vomit. Then my body went into a spasm, a physical wave travelled along my spine and the sick feeling went. After that it was as if I exploded into bliss.

I could feel that my octagonal symbol was now in my heart chakra, and white/golden waves of energy were radiating out of it all over me and all around me. I heard my friend saying "if you want to, you can share what is happening", but when I tried to answer her I found that I couldn't speak. I just about managed to mumble "Hi han't heak..." then I burst out laughing! And I sank back into bliss again. Waves of energy were running all over my body – so high, so pure... and I could see a sort of dashboard in front of me, going from 40% up: 60%, 70%, 80%.... This is it, the process is nearly finished... I lay there bathed in a state of total bliss, and at that moment I knew that we are so much more powerful than we think. I knew that I can live on Prana, I don't need food at all. I knew that I can live to be 200 or 400 years old. We all can do this. We are just conditioned by this society. Because we believe that we live up to around 100 years old this is how old we get. But that is not the truth, the truth is that we can do so much more. And this is a real knowing. It is completely different from a theory, or reading about it, I just *knew* it...

Then all of a sudden I opened my eyes and saw the time: I need to pick Vicky up from school in 15 minutes *(and it's a 20 minute drive)*... Then I heard a voice inside my head "don't worry, go... the process will finish later"... Slowly the energy calmed down and after a little while I could open my eyes again. My friend saw that something big had happened, and offered me two beautifully prepared plates of food to ground myself. One has some nuts – but it's way too heavy, I can't eat that at the moment! The other has some fruit: strawberries, blueberries, grapes, raspberries. The only thing I could eat is the raspberries. They are the lightest, they have the highest frequency. I was completely unable to drive so my friend drove me back to school. Somehow by this time I was able to pick Vicky up and drive her home (*don't ask me how...*)

That day (and the next few days) I was hardly able to function. I remember that I went to the beach to meet with a good friend who had her birthday. When she saw me she said: "wow you had something big happening didn't you?" I told her a bit, and couldn't speak much for the rest of the time. It was too much... That evening I couldn't even eat: my dinner was a glass of barleygrass juice and a tiny piece of chocolate.

Over the next few days I just wanted to be alone, to be in my own energy. I could not be with a group of people, all of a sudden I was too sensitive to other's energy. I was not very hungry. And I longed to meditate. I couldn't wait until it was the evening, when my daughter Vicky was asleep and I had the space to meditate. It felt like I had the same need to meditate that I normally have to eat. I needed it in order to nourish myself. I do meditate regularly, but normally it always feels like a must somehow. I know that it is good for me and that I feel better afterwards, but I need to force myself to do it. But now I really wanted to meditate, I couldn't wait to connect with this pure high energy again!

The next Saturday I did my usual MerKaBa meditation in the morning (*this is a specific meditation technique that is explained in Part Two*). When I finished the MerKaBa meditation I was guided to do certain movements and take a mudra (*hand position)* that is similar to what you see on certain Buddha statues. As I meditated in this way I could feel an energy come in. First there was my own soul energy, but then a different kind of energy came in. I felt a deep peace, and an emptiness, but a full emptiness, a warm emptiness. I can only describe this energy as Buddha energy. The dashboard appears again: 90%... It felt so nice...

I could feel that the energy around me is exactly like you see on certain Buddha images (*see next page*): there is this big sphere of energy around me, coming from my heart, with little waves vibrating through it... Then a smaller sphere around my head, coming from my 3rd eye... At the bottom of my spine my Kundalini field is gently activated and radiates out horizontally – this is the "flowerbed" that the Buddha sits on... For the first time ever, I realised that this picture is a literal depiction of the Buddhafield energy, and not some symbolic portrait.

The next day I could feel all this energy integrating inside me, and when I meditated that evening I saw the dashboard again: 100%. The process was complete.

2
Making sense of it

It took me the whole summer to integrate the experience and to make sense of it. I wrote with my guides: "How did this happen? Why did it happen to me?" as I was not actively searching for it, I was not looking for enlightenment...

They explained that I had experienced two waves: the first wave was emptiness. The second wave was bliss. At the end it merged – the emptiness with the bliss, the full emptiness, the Buddha energy.

Looking back at it, the signs that I received made sense: first I saw two deer, then two toads. Also, at this time my washing machine broke down. I got a new one, but this also broke down after a week. So two new washing machines! In total there had been three signs, as often happens. A beautiful synchronicity. Also the first wave started on the 26th, which is my favourite number. Life is amazing!

I found that my energy had changed a lot. It was a bit like having a new body and finding out what it could do. For example, shortly after the second wave I went to Holland to visit my dad. I drove by car from my home in South England – door to door this was a twelve hour journey, and I had only slept three hours the night before. But when I arrived at my dad's place late in the afternoon the next day I felt completely fine. I didn't feel tired at all. My dad noticed it as well and said "you look really well, did you rest for a while?" But I had travelled non-stop without any breaks. It was so strange, I had done this journey several times and normally I would be exhausted by the time I arrived.

Another example was that when I was in Holland with my daughter, we went to a beach. At some point she said "come dad, let's run for a bit" and she ran off. I started running after her and after a few seconds I felt this rush of energy come in, and all of a sudden I was running without any effort at all. It was as if somebody switched the turbo on and I got a surge of extra power.

But I found out that there was a downside too. A few weeks later I was back home in England. Two good friends were staying with me for a while, and one evening we were all having dinner. At some point they started arguing, and I could feel the energy waves coming at me. It was a much lower frequency than the one I am normally in, and somehow it really affected me. I had to get away from it. Once this frequency, this energy, was in the air I could not be in it (even after they stopped talking). It was really strange, like a complete overload of my system. After a while I had to leave the room and shut myself off by putting on headphones and listening to some music. I am never this sensitive, so I was really shocked by the experience.

A few weeks later something similar happened again. One day at the weekend I was tired, but decided to go to a dancing event in the afternoon. I love music and I love dancing, so I thought it would energise me. It started out ok, but after a while they played a techno song that had a strong piercing electronic sound in it. At least that was what it was like for me. It felt as if all of a sudden they turned the volume up a lot (*I later checked with a friend who was there, but of course they hadn't*). It felt like somebody was drilling into my head with a pneumatic drill... this strong electronic pulse went straight through my skull into my head. And it physically hurt! So I lay down on the floor and tried to close myself down energetically. But no matter what I tried, nothing worked. My head was hurting like mad. Even when the next (calmer) song came my head kept hurting, my senses had gone into overdrive. No matter what I tried, I could not snap out of this state, so I had to leave. Back at home I lay down and had to close the curtains to block out the sunlight. After a long night sleep I was fine again the next morning.

After a few weeks I slowly came out of my "super state" and returned to a more normal state of consciousness. I lost my "super powers" but also I was not over sensitive again.

3
What is Enlightenment?

Enlightenment is said to be the ultimate goal of the spiritual path, indeed the ultimate goal of human life itself. But there is a lot of confusion about what enlightenment is, so before I start talking about enlightenment, let's try to define what it actually is.

The Oxford Dictionary defines enlightenment as: "The action or state of attaining or having attained spiritual knowledge or insight, in particular (in Buddhism) that awareness which frees a person from the cycle of rebirth." This is not a very helpful definition in my view. How do you know when your awareness frees you from rebirth? You will only find out after your death!

So let's have a look at what Wikipedia says: "The English term "enlightenment" is the Western translation of the term Bodhi, "awakening." Bodhi means literally "to have woken up and understood." So here the confusion starts. The terms "awakened" and "enlightened" are used to describe the same state, but I will explain later that there is a difference between the two.

So how do Buddhist define Enlightenment? The Buddhist Master Gelshe Kelsang Gyatso in his book "The Oral Instructions of Mahamudra" says:
"The function of meditation is to give rise to mental peace.
The supreme permanent mental peace is enlightenment.
Mahamudra means the union of great bliss and emptiness.
This union of great bliss and peace is the ultimate enlightenment."

Actually, the word itself contains the meaning: enlightened – the light has come in. This is why emptiness alone is not total enlightenment. Then you are just empty. You need the bliss, the light. But the emptiness creates the space for the light to come in. The simultaneous experience of emptiness and bliss is the ultimate enlightenment.

But I don't want this book to become an academic discussion. So in order to understand enlightenment better and make more tangible what it means to be enlightened, I will look at some of the most well known enlightened masters of this time:
- Yogananda (1895 - 1952)
- Krishnamurti (1895 - 1986)
- Osho (1931 - 1989)
- Papaji (1910 - 1997)
- Andrew Cohen
- Mooji
- Adyashanti
- Eckhart Tolle

In the short chapters below I will describe for each one of them: how they reached enlightenment, and their enlightenment experience itself. Afterwards, I will explain the four possible paths to reach enlightenment, and the difference between being Awakened and being truly Enlightened.

But now let's first look at the stories of the famous ones…

4
Yogananda (1893 – 1952)

Paramahansa Yogananda's *"Autobiography of a Yogi"* is considered to be one of the most influential spiritual works of the 20th century. This book launched thousands of seekers, who were drawn to the promise it makes: Oneness with God is within our reach.

Yogananda was born in 1893 in India. He felt a spiritual calling from a very young age, and found his master (guru) Sri Yukteswar Giri when he was 17. Thus began his education in the art and practice of Kriya Yoga. In Kriya Yoga, energy within the body is manipulated to help bring about a spiritual transformation. Yogananda studied with his master in his hermitage for almost ten years.

Yogananda spent the majority of his life in the United States. He was chosen by his master to bring the Kriya Yoga teaching to the

West. He came to America in 1920, and in the same year founded the *Self-Realisation Fellowship* to disseminate worldwide his teachings on India's ancient science and philosophy of Kriya Yoga. He toured the US extensively, giving lectures to thousands of people. He published his life story *"the Autobiography of a Yogi"* in 1946, and the book became a resounding success. By his death in 1952 he had initiated more than 100,000 disciples into the practice.

Yogananda's enlightenment story

(This is an edited extract from "The Autobiography of a Yogi" by Paramahansa Yogananda)

"I am here, Guruji." My shamefacedness spoke more eloquently for me.

"Let us go to the kitchen and find something to eat." Sri Yukteswar's manner was as casual as though hours and not days had separated us.

"Master, I must have disappointed you by my abrupt departure from my duties here; I thought you might be angry with me."

"No, of course not! Wrath springs only from thwarted desires. I do not expect anything from others, so their actions cannot be in opposition to wishes of mine. I would not use you for my own ends; I am happy only in your own true happiness."

"Sir, one hears of divine love in a vague way, but today I am indeed having a concrete example of it from your angelic self! In the world, even a father does not easily forgive his son if he leaves his parent's business without warning. But you show not the slightest vexation, though you must have been put to great inconvenience by the many unfinished tasks I left behind."

We looked into each other's eyes, where tears were shining. A blissful wave engulfed me; I was conscious that the Lord, in the form of my guru, was expanding the small ardors of my heart into the vast reaches of cosmic love.

A few mornings later I made my way to Master's empty sitting room. I planned to meditate, but my laudable purpose was unshared by disobedient thoughts. They scattered like birds before the hunter.

"Mukunda!" Sri Yukteswar's voice sounded from a distant balcony.

I felt rebellious as my thoughts. "Master always urges me to meditate" I muttered to myself. "He should not disturb me when he knows why I came to his room." He summoned me again; I remained obstinately silent. The third time his tone held rebuke.

"Sir, I am meditating", I shouted protestingly.

"I know how you are meditating", my guru called out, "with your mind distributed like leaves in a storm! Come here to me."

Thwarted and exposed, I made my way sadly to his side.

"Poor boy, mountains cannot give you what you want."

Master spoke caressingly, comfortingly. His calm gaze was unfathomable. "Your heart's desire shall be fulfilled."

Sri Yukteswar seldom indulged in riddles; I was bewildered. He struck gently on my chest above the heart. My body became immovably rooted; breath was drawn out of my lungs as if by some huge magnet. Soul and mind instantly lost their physical bondage and streamed out like a fluid piercing light from my every pore. The flesh was as though dead, yet in my intense awareness I knew that never before had I been fully alive. My sense of identity was no longer narrowly confined to a body but embraced the circumambient atoms. People on distant streets seemed to be moving gently over my own remote periphery. The roots of plants and trees appeared through a dim transparency of the soil; I discerned the inward flow of their sap.

The whole vicinity lay bare before me. My ordinary frontal vision was now changed to a vast spherical sight, simultaneously all-perceptive. Through the back of my head I saw men strolling far down Rai Ghat Lane, and noticed also a white cow that was leisurely approaching. When she reached the open ashram gate, I observed her as though with my two physical eyes. After she had passed behind the brick wall of the courtyard, I saw her clearly still.

All objects within my panoramic gaze trembled and vibrated like quick motion pictures. My body, Master's, the pillared courtyard, the furniture and floor, the trees and sunshine, occasionally became violently agitated, until all melted into a luminescent sea; even as sugar crystals, thrown into a glass of water, dissolve after being shaken. The unifying light alternated with materializations of form, the metamorphoses revealing the law of cause and effect in creation.

An oceanic joy broke upon calm endless shores of my soul. The Spirit of God, I realised, is exhaustless Bliss; His body is countless tissues of light. A swelling glory within me began to envelop towns, continents, the earth, solar and stellar systems, tenuous nebulae, and floating universes. The entire cosmos, gently luminous, like a city seen afar at night, glimmered within the infinitude of my being. The dazzling light beyond the sharply etched global outlines faded slightly at the farthest edges; there I saw a mellow radiance, ever undiminished. It was indescribably subtle; the planetary pictures were formed of a grosser light.

The divine dispersion of rays poured from an Eternal Source, blazing into galaxies, transfigured with ineffable auras. Again and again I saw the beams condense into constellations, then resolve into sheets of transparent flame. By rhythmic reversion, sextillion worlds passed into diaphanous luster, then fire became firmament. I recognised the centre of the empyrean as a point of intuitive perception in my heart. Irradiating splendour issued from my nucleus to every part of the universal structure. Blissful amrita, nectar of immortality, pulsated through me with a quicksilver-like fluidity. The creative voice of God I heard resounding as Aum, the vibration of the Cosmic Motor. All of a sudden the breath returned to my lungs. With a disappointment almost unbearable, I realised that my infinite immensity was lost. Once more I was limited to the humiliating cage of a body, not easily accommodative to the Spirit. Like a prodigal child, I had run away from my macrocosmic home and had imprisoned myself in a narrow microcosm.

My guru was standing motionless before me; I started to prostrate myself at his holy feet in gratitude for his having bestowed on me the experience in cosmic consciousness that I had long passionately sought. He held me upright and said quietly: "You must not get overdrunk with ecstasy. Much work yet remains for you in the world. Come, let us sweep the balcony floor; then we shall walk by the Ganges."

I fetched a broom; Master, I knew, was teaching me the secret of balanced living. The soul must stretch over the cosmogonic abysses while the body performs its daily duties. When Sri Yukteswar and I set out later for a stroll, I was still entranced in unspeakable rapture. I saw our bodies as two astral pictures, moving over a road by the river whose essence was sheer light.

"It is the Spirit of God that actively sustains every form and force in the universe; yet He is transcendental and aloof in the blissful uncreated void beyond the worlds of vibratory phenomena", Master explained. "Those that attain Self-realisation on earth live a similar twofold existence. Conscientiously performing their work in the world, they are yet immersed in an inward beatitude...

A master bestows the divine experience of cosmic consciousness when his disciple, by meditation, has strengthened his mind to a degree where the vast vistas would not overwhelm him. Mere intellectual willingness or open-mindedness is not enough. Only adequate enlargement of consciousness by yoga practice and devotional bhakti can prepare one to absorb the liberating shock of omnipresence.

5
Krishnamurti (1895 – 1986)

The story of Jiddu Krishnamurti is a most unusual one. He was born in 1895 in India. In 1909, when he was fourteen years old, he was discovered on the beach one day by Charles Leadbeater, a leading figure of the Theosophical Society. Leadbeater said that the boy had the most wonderful aura he had ever seen, and predicted that he would become a great spiritual teacher.

The theosophical society was a spiritualist order headed by Annie Besant. It was set up to find the Lord Maitreya (the World Teacher). Theosophists had long been waiting for the reincarnation of Buddha. The ancient texts promised his return where he would appear as the Maitreya – the friend. Theosophists believed that Buddha had not reincarnated because he was unable to find a suitable host and their sole purpose was to find the right host.

Leadbeater became convinced that Krishnamurti would be the perfect vehicle for Lord Maitreya. Krishnamurti was taken under the wing of the Theosophical Society, and was raised and bred to be that perfect host. He was given the best education in England. He was supported and surrounded by some of the world's most advanced spiritual practitioners, receiving advanced occult initiations and training.

In 1922 Krishnamurti had his first awakening experience. He felt unwell, having a severe pain in the nape of his neck, and complained of feeling a terrible heat and was shivering and trembling. After three days like this the people who were looking after him made him sit under a tree in the garden. There he calmed down and had his first "awakening" – everybody present (including Krishnamurti himself) believed that the consciousness of Lord Maitreya was entering his body.

This was the start of "the process", as Krishnamurti called it. On a regular basis he would suffer terrible pains in his body, mainly his neck, head, and base of the spine. This happened mostly during the night, and often he would be unable to do anything during the day. The process started in 1922 and lasted until 1927, sometimes daily, for months at a time. It was assumed that his body was being prepared for the coming of Lord Maitreya.

Two events had a big influence on Krishnamurti. The first was that his brother Nitya became gravely ill. Mrs Besant and Charles Leadbeater assured Krishnamurti that the Masters would not allow him to die, that his life was too important. But despite their assurances Nitya died in 1925.

Another development also happened in 1925. When Charles Leadbeater was away, another member of the theosophical society named George Arundale claimed that he was "bringing through" messages from the Master, that he and a few others had been given further initiations by the Masters, and were chosen to be the "apostles" of Lord Maitreya. Krishnamurti and Leadbeater strongly rejected all of these happenings, and it caused a rift at the top of the Theosophical society.

By 1927 Krishnamurti claimed that his consciousness had now blended with that of Lord Maitreya. In a speech he declared:
"I am one with the beloved, I have found what I longed for, I have become united, so that henceforth there will be no separation, because my thoughts, my desires, my longings – those of the individual self, have been destroyed... Until now you have been depending on the two protectors of the Order (Besant and Leadbeater) for authority, on someone else to tell you the truth, whereas the truth lies within you..."

The speech was a shock to the Theosophists, who were used to step by step instructions and initiations by Leadbeater. But a much bigger shock was to come...

On the 3rd of August 1929 theosophists worldwide gathered in the Netherlands to see the holy vessel that was Jiddu Krishnamurti. It was a meeting of the Order of the Star – an organisation whose sole purpose was to usher in the new era. As thousands sat around him, he shocked his audience by announcing the dissolution of the Order. It was a radical break from his past and a bold affirmation of his own being. Krishnamurti declared:

"Truth is a pathless land, and you cannot approach it by any path whatsoever, by any religion, by any sect... truth cannot be organized; nor should any organization be formed to lead or coerce people along a particular path... I am concerning myself with only one essential thing: to set man free. I desire to free him from all cages, from all fears, and not to found new religions, new sects, nor to establish new theories and new philosophies."

After that speech he dissolved the Order of the Star and returned all the land and assets that were given to the Order (The theosophical society had around 43,000 members and was very affluent). He completely broke with the Theosophical Society, and rejected all their spiritualist practices.

He continued teaching, travelled all around the world, and founded several schools. He tirelessly preached that spiritual enlightenment was at hand for anyone who wanted it. He abhorred all gurus, masters, spiritual practices and religions. The truth was to be found within and nowhere else.

Krishnamurti's enlightenment story

(This is an edited extract from "The life and death of Krishnamurti" by Mary Lutyens)

The morning of the next day (the 20th) was almost the same as the previous day, and I could not tolerate too many people in the room. I could feel them in rather a curious way and their vibrations got on my nerves. That evening at about the same hour of six I felt worse than ever. I wanted nobody near me nor anybody to touch me. I was feeling extremely tired and weak. I think I was weeping from mere exhaustion and lack of physical control. My head was pretty bad and the top part felt as though many needles were being driven in. While I was in this state I felt that the bed in which I was lying, the same one as on the previous day, was dirty and filthy beyond imagination and I could not lie in it.

All of a sudden I found myself sitting on the floor and Nitya and Rosalind asking me to get into bed. I asked them not to touch me and cried out that the bed was not clean. I went on like this for some time till eventually I wandered out on the veranda and sat a few moments exhausted and slightly calmer. I began to come to myself and finally Mr. Warrington asked me to go under the pepper tree which is near the house.

There I sat crosslegged in the meditation posture. When I had sat thus for some time, I felt myself going out of my body, I saw myself sitting down with the delicate tender leaves of the tree over me. I was facing the east. In front of me was my body and over my head I saw the Star, bright and clear.

Then I could feel the vibrations of the Lord Buddha; I beheld Lord Maitreya and Master Kuthumi. I was so happy, calm and at peace. I could still see my body and I was hovering near it. There was such profound calmness both in the air and within myself, the calmness of the bottom of a deep unfathomable lake. Like the lake, I felt my physical body, with its mind and emotions, could be ruffled on the surface but nothing, nay nothing, could disturb the calmness of my soul.

The presence of the mighty Beings was with me for some time and then they were gone. I was supremely happy, for I had seen. Nothing could ever be the same. I have drunk at the clear and pure waters at the source of the fountain of life and my thirst was appeased. Never more could I be thirsty, never more could I be in utter darkness. I have seen the Light. I have touched compassion which heals all sorrow and suffering; it is not for myself, but for the world. I have stood on the mountain top and gazed at the mighty Beings. Never can I be in utter darkness; I have seen the glorious and healing light. The fountain of Truth has been revealed to me and the darkness has been dispersed. Love in all its glory has intoxicated my heart; my heart can never be closed. I have drunk at the fountain of joy and eternal beauty. I am God-intoxicated.

6
Osho (1931 – 1989)

Osho was previously known as Bhagwan Shree Rajneesh during the 1970's and 1980's, and took the name Osho in 1989 (*meaning "ocean of wisdom"*). Osho is perhaps the most controversial spiritual teacher there has ever been. He has been described as "the most dangerous man that lived since Jesus Christ." Who was Osho? Was he the "Master of Masters", a great being that incarnated to advance human understanding? Or was he just another self-important guru out for fame and fortune?

Osho was born in 1931 in a small rural village in India. His parents let him live with his maternal grandparents until he was seven years old. By his own account, this was a major influence on his development because his grandmother gave him the utmost freedom, leaving him carefree without any imposed education or restrictions. When he was seven years old, his grandfather died, and he returned to live with his parents. There he enrolled in school for the first time. When he was not creating mischief and challenging his teachers, Osho continued the adventurous and often solitary approach to life that characterised his first years with his grandparents. When he turned 14 he undertook a seven-day experiment in waiting for death, provoked in part by a prediction of an astrologer who predicted that "it is almost certain that this child will die at twenty-one. Every seven years he will face death."

When Osho was 21 he reached enlightenment. But he did not tell anyone about this, he remained quiet and deepened his experience. He studied philosophy at University and won numerous awards in debating competitions.

He started teaching philosophy at University, and attended public speaking engagements throughout India. Osho, then known as Bhagwan Shree Rajneesh, took India by storm. He travelled to and fro, giving speeches and stirring up controversy wherever he went. His university training as a professional debater proved invaluable. None could match him. His reputation grew.

Osho quickly gathered a large following, and started his first meditation centres in 1962. Known as the "rich man's guru", he proclaimed Indian socialism misguided. He decried Gandhi's obsession with poverty and suffering. Unlike many of his spiritual peers, he pushed for a capitalistic-scientific revolution that would allow everyone to shake off the shackles of poverty. Only from a position of wealth and comfort would the majority of people begin the return to God. When everything you've accumulated no longer makes you happy, you begin to ask the great questions: Who am I? Why am I here? Where am I from? And where am I going?

In 1968 he gave a series of talks that were published in the book "From Sex to Superconsciousness." In it he advocated that one should not repress sexual desire, and called for a freer acceptance of sex. This caused a great controversy, and he got labelled as a "Sex Guru."

Unlike Krishnamurti, who was another popular spiritual teacher at the time, Osho saw the master-disciple relationship as an effective tool that a seeker could use to facilitate his or her self-realisation. Intense love and devotion to the master (*a form of Bhakti practice*), allowed the seeker to transcend the mind and experience a greater union with life.

In 1974 he started his first community in Pune. Thousands of people would come to stay there. More and more Westerners found their way to his ashram, and tensions with the government were mounting. As a result he moved to Oregon in the United States in 1981 and set up a new commune there. The authorities did not want him there, and a legal battle began that went on for years. During this time Osho gathered a collection of 93 Rolls-Royces, and bitter arguments with the local establishment were going on.

The Oregon commune collapsed in 1985 when Osho called in the FBI and revealed that the commune leadership had committed a number of serious crimes, including a bio-terror attack (food contamination) on local citizens. Osho was arrested shortly afterwards and charged with immigration violations. For twelve days he was driven from one prison to another, then finally he was deported from the country.

Osho looked for a new place to live, and travelled around the world as twenty-one countries denied him entry. He eventually returned to India, and continued teaching in 1986 at his Pune commune. His health quickly deteriorated however, and Osho's doctors claimed that he was poisoned during the twelve days he was imprisoned. Osho died in 1989.

Osho's enlightenment story

(This is an edited extract from "Autobiography of a Spiritually Incorrect Mystic" by Osho)

In the last year, when I was twenty-one, it was a time of nervous breakdown and breakthrough. I was so different from other children. I sat by the bank of the river and went on looking at the sky for hours, sometimes the whole night. Most people thought I was mad. That one year was tremendous. I was surrounded with nothingness, emptiness. I had lost all contact with the world. If somebody reminded me to take a bath, I would go on taking a bath for hours. Then they had to knock on the door: "now come out of the bathroom." If they reminded me to eat I ate, otherwise days would pass and I would not eat.

My whole concern was to go deeper and deeper into myself. And the pull was so magnetic, so immense, like what physicists now call black holes. That one year of tremendous pull drew me farther and farther away from people, so much so that I would not recognise my own mother. There were times I forgot my own name. Naturally, to everybody else during that one year I was mad. But to me that madness became meditation, and the peak of that madness opened the door. I was simply lying, sitting, walking – deep down there was no doer. I had lost all ambition, there was no desire to be anybody, no desire to reach. I was simply thrown into myself. It was an emptiness, and emptiness drives one crazy. But emptiness is the only door to God.

To me it happened in a state of total relaxation. I had tried everything. And then, seeing the futility of all my effort, I said: Enough is enough. And I forgot the whole project. I forgot it forever. For seven days I lived as ordinarily as possible.

On the day the search stopped, the day I was not seeking for something, the day I was not expecting something to happen – it started happening. A new energy arose – out of nowhere. It was not coming from any source. It was coming from nowhere and everywhere. This new energy was a new light and a new delight, it became so intense that it was almost unbearable – as if I was exploding, as if I was going mad with blissfulness. This was so alive, it was like a tidal wave of bliss. The whole day was strange, stunning, and it was a shattering experience. The past was disappearing as if it had never belonged to me, as if I had dreamed about it, as if it was someone else's story. I was becoming loose from my past, I was becoming a non-being, what Buddha calls Anatta, boundaries were disappearing, distinctions were disappearing. Mind was disappearing, it was a million miles away. It was difficult to catch hold of it, it was rushing further and further away and there was no urge to keep it close. I was simply indifferent about it all. By the evening it became so difficult to bear it – it was hurting, it was painful. My eyes were closing, it was difficult to keep them open. Something was imminent, something was going to happen. It was difficult to say what it was – maybe it was going to be my death – but there was no fear. I was ready for it. Around 8pm I went to sleep. It was a very strange sleep. The body was asleep, I was awake. It was so strange – as if one is torn apart in two directions. Sleep and awareness were meeting, death and life were meeting. That is the moment when you can say that the creator and the creation meet. It was weird. It shook me to the very roots. You can never be the same after that experience; it brings a new vision to your life, a new quality.

Around midnight my eyes all of a sudden opened – I had not opened them, the sleep was broken by something else. I felt a great presence around me in the room. I felt throbbing life all around me, great vibration – almost like a hurricane, a great storm of light, joy, ecstasy. I was drowning in it. It was so tremendously real that everything else became unreal. The walls of the room became unreal, the house became unreal, my own body became unreal. Everything was unreal because now there was, for the first time, reality. A deep urge arose in me to rush out of the room, to go under the sky – it was suffocating me. It was too much! It will kill me! I rushed out of the room, and immediately as I came out, the feeling of being suffocated disappeared. I walked towards the nearest garden, I was walking, or I was running, or I was flying, it was difficult to decide. There was no gravitation, I was feeling weightless – as if some energy was taking me. I was in the hands of some other energy. For the first time I was not alone, for the first time I was no more an individual, for the first time, the drop had fallen in the ocean. Now the whole ocean was mine, I was the ocean. There was no limitation. A tremendous power arose as if I could do anything whatsoever. I was not there, only the power was there.

I reached the garden where I used to go every day. The moment I entered the garden everything became luminous, it was all over the place – the benediction, the blessedness. I could see the trees for the first time – their green, their life, their very sap running. The whole garden was asleep, the trees were asleep. But I could see the whole garden alive, even the small grass leaves were so beautiful. I looked around. One tree was tremendously luminous – the maulshree tree. It attracted me, it pulled me towards itself. I had not chosen it, God himself has chosen it. I went to the tree, I sat under the tree. As I sat there things started settling. The whole universe became a benediction.

That day something happened that has continued – not as a continuity, but it has still happened as an undercurrent. Not as a permanency – each moment it has been happening again and again. It has been a miracle each moment. And since that night I have never been in the body. I am hovering around it. I became tremendously powerful and at the same time very fragile. I became very strong, the strength that is of a rose flower, so fragile, so sensitive, so delicate.

Each moment I am surprised I am still here, I should not be. I should have left any moment. Still I am here. Every morning I open my eyes and I say "So, again I am still here?" Because it seems almost impossible. The miracle has been a continuity.

7
Papaji (1910 – 1997)

Papaji (also known as H.L. Poonja) may not have such a big name as Yogananda or Osho, but he is the Guru of arguably some of the most popular enlightened teachers of this time: Andrew Cohen, Mooji, and Gangaji.

Papaji was born in 1910 in India. When he was eight years old he had a mystical experience. One day when his mother handed him a mango drink, he could make no movement to grasp it. He had all of a sudden fallen into a deep mystical trance. So deep was the trance that all attempts to shake him out of it failed. He stayed in this state for two full days. Thinking that he was possessed the panicked family took him to the local mosque and asked the mullah to perform an exorcism. But nothing worked. Eventually when he came out of his trance, he was unable to say much about it except that he had an "intensely happy" experience and he had experienced "unfathomable beauty and peace."

His mother was convinced that his trance was somehow related to Lord Krishna, and convinced him to start meditating on Krishna. So strong was his desire to return to the state that he had experienced, that he began to meditate intensely on the child form of Krishna. Soon the child-Krishna began appearing before him when he was alone at night.

At sixteen Papaji had another deep mystical experience, similar to the one he had when he was eight. This time the experience was triggered by the invocation of the prayer: Om Shanti, Shanti! (Om Peace, Peace!) This happened when he was at school and it left him completely immobile. His schoolmates made fun of him and carried him around in his paralyzed state, and when they tired of it, they dumped him at his home. All through this experience, Papaji was in a deep state of bliss but unable to move or respond. He was now convinced that his experience was as a result of his devotion to Krishna and his devotion considerably deepened as a result.

Because of his deep spiritual tendencies and his deep devotion to Krishna, he did not do well at school and as a result could not go to college. Instead, at the age of eighteen he became a travelling salesman and got married at the age of twenty. Though he was not interested in marriage he got married on insistence of his father who also selected the bride for him. In due course he became the father of a son and a daughter.

After several years he began wandering the country in search of Gurus who could help him. He met many great spiritual teachers, but none could help him and he returned home empty handed. Shortly after he returned home a wandering monk (Sadhu) appeared at his home. Papaji invited him in and offered him food. He then asked him, "Can you show me God? If not, do you know anyone who can?" To his surprise the monk told him that he should go to meet the sage Ramana Maharishi and that he would show him God. He then gave him explicit directions how to get there.

Some time later, when he reached the hermitage where Ramana Maharishi stayed, he was shocked to see that Ramana Maharishi was none other than the same man who had visited his home. He was disgusted at this and made preparations to leave without meeting the sage. He thought: "Ramana Maharishi visits my home, advertises himself and then jumps back on a train to reach here before me! How disgusting! He is nothing but a fraud who wanders the country advertising himself."

Just as he was leaving he ran into somebody who convinced him to stay. He assured him that Ramana Maharishi had never left town for the past forty-eight years. His curiosity aroused Papaji decided to stay and meet the sage.

When he eventually met Ramana Maharishi he was very aggressive. He asked him repeatedly if he had come to his house, but he got no answer from the sage. Eventually he asked Ramana Maharishi to show him God. To this query the sage replied, "No. I cannot show you God or enable you to see God, because God is not an object to be seen. God is the subject. He is the seer. Don't concern yourself with objects that can be seen. Find out who the seer is." He then added, "You alone are God!"

Just when the sage stopped speaking Papaji felt his entire body tremble and shake. His nerve endings felt as if they were dancing and his hair stood on end. He later described the experience as an opening of the spiritual heart, "It was as if a bud inside opened up and bloomed. And when I say 'Heart' I don't mean that the flowering was located in a particular place in the body. This Heart, this Heart of my Heart, was neither inside the body nor out of it. I can't give a more exact description of what happened. All I can say is that in the Maharishi's presence, and under his gaze, the Heart opened and bloomed. It was an extraordinary experience, one that I had never had before. I had not come looking for any kind of experience, so it totally surprised me when it happened."

Even though he had this extraordinary experience he was somehow not impressed with Ramana Maharishi. All his life he had spent being devoted to Krishna and getting his visions. He was unable to grasp how nobody in this hermitage including the sage himself was devoted to Krishna in the manner he expected them to be. He expected everybody to be continuously chanting the name of

Krishna like he did. Eventually he left the place disappointed and reported back to work.

He would get up at 2.30 am every morning and repeat the name of Krishna till 9.30 am. Then he would proceed to work. Once he came back from work he would once again lock himself in the room where he did his meditation and resume his chanting. His goal was to repeat the name of Krishna at least fifty thousand times during the day.
Then one day something bewildering happened. At 2.30 am he had a vision of Lord Rama, his wife Sita, his brother Lakshmana, and his great disciple Hanumana. The vision lasted 7 hours till 9.30 am. He then went to work but when he came back he was unable to resume his chanting of Krishna. He was unable to read any spiritual books either. This left him bewildered. Why had Rama appeared before him rather than Krishna? Why could he not chant the name of Krishna as he did before? What happened?

He began visiting all the holy men in his town to get an answer, but he was disappointed, as no one provided him with a satisfactory explanation. Then he had a vision of the sage Ramana Maharishi standing before him and smiling. This gave him the thought that he should visit the sage and maybe he could provide him with a solution to his dilemma.

When he met the Maharishi he said, "For twenty-five years I have been repeating the name of Krishna. Up till fairly recently I was managing 50,000 repetitions a day. I also used to read a lot of spiritual literature. Then Rama, Sita, Lakshmana and Hanuman appeared before me. After they left, I couldn't carry on with my practice. I can't repeat the name any more. I can't read my books. I can't meditate. I feel very quiet inside but there is no longer any desire in me to put my attention on God. In fact, I can't do it even if I try. My mind refuses to engage itself in thoughts of God. What has happened to me and what should I do?"

The Maharshi looked at him and asked, "How did you come here?"

He did not see the point of this question but politely said, "By train."

"And what happened when you got to the station?" the sage inquired.

"Well, I got off the train, handed in my ticket and engaged a bullock cart to bring me here."

"And when you reached here and paid off the driver of the cart, what happened to the cart?"

"It went away, presumably back to town," he replied, still not clear as to where this line of questioning was leading.

The Maharishi then explained what he was driving at, "The train brought you to your destination. You got off it because you didn't need it anymore. It had brought you to the place you wanted to reach. Likewise with the bullock cart. You got off it when it had brought you here. You don't need either the train or the cart any more. They were the means for bringing you here. Now you are here, they are of no use to you. That is what has happened with your chanting, your reading, and your meditation. They have brought you to your spiritual destination. You don't need them anymore. You yourself did not give up your practices, they left you of their own accord because they had served their purpose. You have arrived."

What happened next is described by Papaji as follows: "Then he looked at me intently. I could feel that my whole body and mind were being washed with waves of purity. They were being purified by his silent gaze. I could feel him looking intently into my heart. Under that spellbinding gaze I felt every atom of my body being purified. It was as if a new body was being created for me. A process of transformation was going on—the old body was dying, atom by atom, and a new body was being created in its place. Then, all of a sudden, I understood. I knew that this man who had spoken to me was, in reality, what I already was, what I had always been. There was a sudden impact of recognition as I became aware of the Self."

"I use the word 'recognition' deliberately, because as soon as the experience was revealed to me, I knew, unerringly, that this was the same state of peace and happiness that I had been immersed in as an eight-year-old boy in Lahore, on the occasion when I had refused to accept the mango drink. The silent gaze of the Maharishi re-established me in that primal state, but this time it was permanent. The 'I' which had for so long been looking for a God outside of itself, because it wanted to get back to that original childhood state, perished in the direct knowledge and experience of the Self which the Maharishi revealed to me. I cannot describe exactly what the experience was or is because the books are right when they say that words cannot convey it. I can only talk about peripheral things. I can say that every cell, every atom in my body leapt to attention as they all recognised and experienced the Self that animated and supported them, but the experience itself I cannot describe. I knew that my spiritual quest had definitely ended, but the source of that knowledge will always remain indescribable. I got up and prostrated to the Maharishi in gratitude. I had finally understood what his teachings were and are."

After his realisation experience Papaji wanted to stay with Maharishi and was very reluctant to return back to work, but he had a family to feed. So after a few days, he reluctantly took leave of his Guru and returned back to work. What was remarkable for Papaji was that his mind had become completely "thoughtless" and he did not need thoughts to function. This is what he said later:

"In the first few months after my realisation, I didn't have a single thought. I could go to the office and perform all my duties without ever having a thought in my head. There was an ocean of inner silence that never gave rise to even a ripple of thought. It did not take me long to realise that a mind and thoughts are not necessary to function in the world. When one abides as the Self, some divine power takes charge of one's life. All actions then take place spontaneously, and are performed very efficiently, without any mental effort or activity."

Papaji was happy. He had found Self-realisation and he had found a true guru. But in 1947, due to growing tensions between Hindus and Muslims in India, Maharishi requested him to get his family to India so that they would be safe. Papaji did so, and he had to work hard night and day to take care of his family. Papaji was a householder saint and never shrank away from his responsibilities. Being established in his Self, he carried out his duties and took care of his responsibilities.

Slowly the fame of this humble householder saint spread. He retired in 1966 and he came to be known as "Papaji." With more time on his hands, he was able to meet more people and his fame spread to other countries. Soon visitors from West began to show up at his doorstep. Amongst his prominent Western disciples are Mooji, Andrew Cohen, and Gangaji.

Papaji died in 1997 after a brief illness.

8
Andrew Cohen

Andrew Cohen was born in New York City in 1955, in an upper-middle class Jewish household. He was a very popular teacher in the US in the 90's and 00's. In 1991 Cohen founded "What is Enlightenment?" magazine (later renamed "EnlightenNext"), which established Cohen as a major contemporary spiritual figure. The magazine ceased being publishing in 2011.

From 2001 he became more and more controversial due to the demands he placed on his students. He stopped teaching in 2013 and declared that he was not enlightened. I decided to include his biography here because it perfectly illustrates some of the problems with enlightenment.

Cohen recounts that his life was changed by a spontaneous experience of "cosmic consciousness" at the age of sixteen. After pursuing a career as a jazz-musician, he began a spiritual quest to recover this experience when he was 22. He eventually met Papaji in 1986, who taught that no effort is needed to attain enlightenment "because it is merely the realisation of what one already is." At their first meeting, Cohen realised that he "had always been free." Papaji declared Cohen to be his heir. Cohen began to teach and gathered a community around him.

Within a few years, Cohen noticed that the ecstatic experiences his students had in his presence were limited. Being convinced that he himself was fully free from karmic bondage, he began to demand more commitment from his students, insisting on complete "ego-transcendence." This change in teaching-style led to dissent amongst the students.

Cohen also broke with Papaji, who was regarded by Cohen as shortcoming in ethical and enlightened behaviour. According to Cohen: "Papaji insisted that the realisation of the Self had nothing to do with worldly behaviour. Papaji did not believe that fully transcending the ego was possible. Karmic tendencies remained after enlightenment, but the enlightened person was no longer identified with them and, therefore, did not accrue further karmic consequences. For Papaji, ethical standards were based on a dualistic understanding of reality and the notion of an individual agent, and therefore were not indicative of non-dual enlightenment."
Cohen did not agree, insisting instead on "flawless behaviour" as the manifestation of enlightenment.

After the break with Papaji, Cohen's teachings were further developed into "Evolutionary Enlightenment", aiming at an impersonal enlightenment which transcends the personal. Yet, the change in teachings-style led also to "physical force, verbal abuse, and intense psychological pressure against students." The growing complaints from students have been described in several publications from former students and from his own mother.

In June 2013, Cohen announced on his blog that he would be taking "a sabbatical for an extended period of time", after confrontational exchanges with his closest students, who helped Cohen to realise, as he put it, that "in spite of the depth of my awakening, my ego is still alive and well."

In May 2015 Cohen posted an extensive apology letter to his former students on his blog, his first writing after emerging from the two-year sabbatical. He wrote about the need to embrace the spiritual principle of agape (the highest form of love), and expresses regret for the ways in which his lack of agape in his teaching methods has hurt and alienated many former students.

9
Mooji

Anthony Paul Moo-Young, known as Mooji, was born on 29 January 1954 in Port Antonio, Jamaica. In 1969, he moved to the UK and lived in Brixton, London. Anthony worked in London's 'West End' as a street portrait artist for many years, then as a painter and a stained glass artist, and later as a teacher at Brixton College. For a long time, he was well known as Tony Moo, but is now affectionately known as Mooji.

In 1987, a chance meeting with a Christian mystic was to be a life-changing encounter for Mooji. He remembers:

"'He initially came asking about my stained glass work and then we'd get talking about Christianity and I felt guided by him. Then one time I asked if he'd pray for me, and he did, one hand on my head. When he was finished, I found myself saying, "Please help me, please guide me." And a profound change occurred; from the next day, I felt strangely more sensitive, like a greater clarity and awareness and a feeling inside of lightness and relaxed excitement."

Within a short period, he experienced a radical shift in consciousness so profound that outwardly he seemed, to many who knew him, to be an entirely different person. As his spiritual consciousness awakened, a deep inner transformation began which unfolded in the form of many miraculous experiences and mystical insights. He felt a strong wind of change blowing through his life which brought with it a deep urge to surrender completely to divine will. Shortly after, he stopped teaching, left his home and began a life of quiet simplicity and surrender to the will of God as it manifested spontaneously within him. A great peace entered his being, and has remained ever since.

For the following six years, Mooji drifted in a state of spontaneous meditation oblivious to the outer world he formally knew. During these years, he lived almost penniless but was constantly absorbed in inner joy, contentment and natural meditation. Grace came in the form of his sister Julianne, who welcomed Mooji into her home with loving kindness, and afforded him the time and space he much needed to flower spiritually, without the usual pressures and demands of external life. Mooji refers to this period of his life as his "wilderness years" and speaks touchingly of a deep feeling of being "seated on the Lap of God." In many respects, these were far from easy times for Mooji, yet there is no trace of regret or remorse in his tone as he recounts these years. On the contrary, he speaks of this phase of his life as being richly blessed and abundant in grace, trust and loving devotion.

In 1993, Mooji travelled to India. He had a desire to visit Dakshineswar in Calcutta where Sri Ramakrishna, the great Bengali Saint, had lived and taught. The words and life of Ramakrishna were a source of inspiration and encouragement to Mooji in the early years of his spiritual development. He loved the Saint deeply but as fate would determine, he would not go to Calcutta. While in

Rishikesh, a holy place at the foothills of the Himalayas, he was to have another auspicious encounter; this time with three devotees of Papaji. Their persistent invitation to Mooji to travel with them to meet the master made a deep impression on him.

In late November 1993, Mooji travelled to Indira Nagar in Lucknow to meet Papaji. It was to be an auspicious and profoundly significant experience on his spiritual journey. He felt it to be his good fortune; he had met a living Buddha, a fully enlightened master. He gradually came to recognise that Papaji was his Guru. Mooji stayed with Papaji for several months. During one particular satsang meeting, Papaji told him: "If you desire to be one with truth, 'you' must completely disappear." On hearing this, great anger arose within his mind, full of judgement and resistance towards Papaji. He decided to leave the master's presence for good, but later that day a huge dark cloud of anger and rebelliousness suddenly lifted, leaving his mind in a state of such peace, emptiness and a love towards the master so intense, that he knew he could not leave. Through 'Papaji's' grace, his mind was pushed back into the emptiness of source.

In 1994 Mooji received news from London that his eldest son had died all of a sudden of pneumonia. He returned to England. The bliss of earlier years gave way to a profound emptiness and inner silence, imparted by the grace and presence of Papaji.

Returning home from India, he started to sell incense in Brixton market 'in a detached kind of energy'. People started to pick up on his wisdom. He would write *"Thought for the Day"* sayings, giving them freely to thousands. People brought him their concerns and he would invite them back for tea. He started to draw a crowd, people came with friends. And when a woman visiting from Ireland invited him to attend her meditation group, his first formal Satsangs began in Ireland.

(Satsang is a Sanskrit term which literally means "gathering together with the truth." In Satsang a group of people sit with a Guru and discuss spiritual teachings and wisdom.)

10
Adyashanti

Steven Gray was born in 1962 in the United States in the San Francisco Bay Area. At age 19 he found the "idea of enlightenment" in a book. Subsequently, he built a hut in his parents' backyard and started practicing meditation. In his 20s, Gray studied Zen Buddhism under the guidance of his Zen teacher Arvis Joen Justi for fourteen years. At age 25 he began experiencing a series of transformative spiritual awakenings. While sitting alone on his cushion, Gray had a classic Kensho, or awakening experience, in which in his own words he: "penetrated to the emptiness of all things and realised that the Buddha I had been chasing was what I was." Besides spending many hours in meditation and prayer, he also studied books about Christian mystics and the Gospels.

For the next few years he continued his meditation practice, while also working at his father's machine shop. In addition to sitting, he spent a lot of time in coffee shops, using journaling as a means of liberating himself from his mind. He would spend hours deliberating over his deepest thoughts and feelings. This requires radical honesty and a certain amount of courage. Our greatest demons are found within. Not all seekers are ready to face them.

Finally, at 31, Gray had an experience of awakening that put to rest all his questions and doubts. In 1996, he was invited to teach by Arvis Joen Justi. He first started giving talks to small gatherings, in a room above his aunt's garage, which grew over the years and he changed his name to "Adyashanti", a Sanskrit term for "primordial peace." Adyashanti's talks focus on awakening and embodying awakening. He downplays his affiliation with Zen. "The Truth I point to is not confined within any religious point of view, belief system, or doctrine, but is open to all and found within all."

Adyashanti's enlightenment story

(This is an edited extract from www.adyashanti.org)

Question: How did awakening and liberation occur for you?
I had my first what traditionally would be called awakening experience when I was 25 years old. This was very powerful and full of emotion and release and joy and bliss and all that it is supposed to be full of. But, because there was so much emotion involved, it obscured the simplicity of awakeness itself. Like so many others, I continued to chase certain ideas and concepts of what awakeness was supposed to be. That caused years of misery.

Gradually over time I had the same experience reoccur, but each time with less and less emotion. I could see more and more clearly over time what was the actual essential element. Then finally an awakening occurred where at the moment of awakening, there was no emotion in it. It was just the pure seeing of what is. When there was the pure seeing of what is, unclouded by emotional content, it was obvious. It was very obvious that consciousness recognised itself for what it really is – aware space before any emotion or thought or manifestation.

Question: Would you say that this is the point at which the distinction between awakening and liberation occurred?
No. Even though there was a freedom and incredible sense of fearlessness and release from not being confined to the dream of a separate "I", I started to feel somewhat discontented with that. I didn't know why I felt discontented, and it didn't bother me in any way. The discontent didn't touch that freedom, so it didn't bother me, but I was interested in it.

Then one day I was sitting reading a book, and I folded the book to put it away and realised that somewhere in some magic time, something had dropped away, and I didn't know what it was. There was just a big absence of something. I went through the rest of the day as usual but noticing some big absence. Then when I sat down on the bed that night, it suddenly hit me that what had fallen away was all identity.

All identity had collapsed, as both the self in the ego sense of a separate me, and as the slightest twinge of identity with the Absolute Self, with the Oneness of consciousness. There had still been some unconscious, identity or "me-ness" which was the cause of the discontent. And it all collapsed. Identity itself collapsed, and from that point on there was no grasping whatsoever for little me or for the unified consciousness me. Identity just fell away and blew away with the wind.

Question: When you noticed that the identity had collapsed and was gone, what remained?
Everything just as it always had been. There was just the lack of any "I", personal or universal, or the fundamental unconscious belief in any identity or of fixating self in any place. The mind can continue to fixate a subtle identity of self even in universal consciousness, or Self. It can be so incredibly easy to miss. To say "I am That" can be a very subtle fixation of consciousness.

Question: It's still a landing, a form of identity?
It's a slight landing, a slight grasping. It's very subtle. But when it collapses, you are even beyond "I am That." You are in a place that cannot be described.

Question: And that is what you call liberation?
That is what I call liberation. Really, in the end, what you end up with is that you don't know who you are. You end up in the same place you started out. You truly don't know who you are because it's impossible to fixate the self anywhere.

11
Eckhart Tolle

Eckhart Tolle was born in Germany in 1948. He was a troubled young man endlessly tormented by his thoughts. He moved to Spain when he was 13, and left school to escape a hostile environment. Distancing himself from his own thinking would prove harder. He occasionally considered suicide to end an existence that he considered meaningless and without purpose.

At the age of 19, Eckhart moved to London to become a language teacher and, eventually, a scholar at Cambridge. However he remained deeply unhappy. Shortly after his 29th birthday, he had a deep transformative enlightenment experience. He realised his true spiritual nature and was finally able to distance himself from his poisonous thoughts. The power of awareness in the "now" remains his core teaching.

He spent the following years deepening his understanding while living a marginal life in London. Unemployed and homeless, he had a habit of sitting on park benches and blissfully watching the world go by. After several years he started reading spiritual texts and spent time with spiritual teachers, and slowly started working with others. His experiences in teaching others led to him writing *"The Power of Now"*, published in 1997, which catapulted him to one of the most influential spiritual teachers of this time.

Echkart Tolle's enlightenment story

(This is an edited extract from "The Power of Now" by Eckhart Tolle)

Until my thirtieth year, I lived in a state of almost continuous anxiety interspersed with periods of suicidal depression. It feels now as if I am talking about some past lifetime or somebody else's life.

One night not long after my twenty-ninth birthday, I woke up in the early hours with a feeling of absolute dread. I had woken up with such a feeling many times before, but this time it was more intense than it had ever been. The silence of the night, the vague outlines of the furniture in the dark room, the distant noise of a passing train - everything felt so alien, so hostile, and so utterly meaningless, that it created in me a deep loathing of the world. The most loathsome thing of all, however, was my own existence. What was the point in continuing to live with this burden of misery? Why carry on with this continuous struggle? I could feel that a deep longing for annihilation, for non-existence, was now becoming much stronger than the instinctive desire to continue to live.

"I cannot live with myself any longer." This was the thought that kept repeating itself in my mind. Then all of a sudden I became aware of what a peculiar thought it was. "Am I one or two? If I cannot live with myself, there must be two of me: the 'I' and the 'self' that 'I' cannot live with." "Maybe", I thought, "only one of them is real." I was so stunned by this strange realisation that my mind stopped. I was fully conscious, but there were no more thoughts. Then I felt drawn into what seemed like a vortex of energy. It was a slow movement at first and then accelerated. I was gripped by an intense fear, and my body started to shake. I heard the words "resist nothing", as if spoken inside my chest. I could feel myself being sucked into a void. It felt as if the void was inside myself rather than outside. All of a sudden, there was no more fear, and I let myself fall into that void. I have no recollection of what happened after that.

I was awakened by the chirping of a bird outside the window. I had never heard such a sound before. My eyes were still closed and I saw the image of a precious diamond. Yes, if a diamond could still make a sound, this is what it would be like. I opened my eyes. The first light of dawn was filtering through the curtains. Without any thought, I felt, I knew, that there is infinitely more to light than we realise. That soft luminosity filtering through the curtains was love itself. Tears came into my eyes. I got up and walked around the room. I recognised the room, and yet I knew that I had never truly seen it before. Everything was fresh and pristine, as if it had just come into existence. I picked up things, a pencil, an empty bottle, marvelling at the beauty and aliveness of it all.

That day I walked around the city in utter amazement at the miracle of life on earth, as if I had just been born into this world.
For the next five months I lived in a state of uninterrupted deep peace and bliss.
A time came when, for a while, I was left with nothing on the physical plane. I had no relationships, no job, no home, no socially defined identity. I spent almost two years sitting on park benches in a state of the most intense joy.

But even the most beautiful experiences come and go. More fundamental, perhaps, than any experience is the undercurrent of peace that has never left me since. Sometimes it is very strong, almost palpable, and others can feel it too. At other times, it is somewhere in the background, like a distant melody.

12
Understanding Enlightenment

There are many questions around enlightenment. Is Andrew Cohen enlightened or not? Are people like Adyashanti and Eckhart Tolle truly enlightened? How enlightened do you have to be to be called enlightened? And what is the difference between being Awakened and being Enlightened? In this chapter I will try to give some clarity.

The question "how enlightened do you have to be to be called enlightened?" has been answered by Buddhists long ago. The Theravada school of Buddhism defines fours levels of enlightenment, as follows: (*source: Wikipedia*)

A Sotapanna (stream enterer) is free of:
- Identity view
- Attachment to rites and rituals
- Doubt about the teachings

> The first stage is that of Sotapanna , literally meaning "one who enters the stream", with the stream being the Noble Eightfold Path regarded as the highest Dharma (teaching).

A Sakadagami (once-returner) has greatly attenuated (reduced):
- Sensual desire
- Ill will

The once-returner will at most return to the realm of the senses one more time. The stream-enterer and once-returner are distinguished by the fact that the once-returner has weakened lust, hate, and delusion to a greater degree.

An Anagami (non-returner) is free from:
- Sensual desire
- Ill will

The non-returner, having overcome sensuality, does not return to the human world after death. Instead, non-returners are reborn in one of the five special worlds called "Pure Abodes", and there attain Nirvana.

An Arahant is free from all of the five lower fetters (*something that restrains*) and the five higher fetters, which are:
- Craving for fine material existence
- Craving for existence on the level of formlessness
- Conceit
- Restlessness
- Ignorance

An Arahant is a fully awakened person. He has abandoned all ten fetters and, upon death will never be reborn in any plane or world.

The difference between Awakened and Enlightened

To keep things a bit more simple (and use Western terms), I would like to simplify this to the following two levels: Awakened and Enlightened.

Awakened:
A person who is awakened is free of identity view (ego) and attachments. There is still an ego, or I-identity, but you are not identified with the Ego. At this stage you still experience emotions, and still have (sensual) desires, but you are not ruled by your senses anymore. Most of the time you will be in a state of mental peace.

Enlightened:
In total enlightenment all form of ego has gone, the ego (self) identity has completely dissolved. All (sensual) desires and any form of cravings have gone. You are in a state of great bliss and emptiness. You are in a permanent state of supreme mental peace. You are one with source.

So who is truly enlightened?

With the above definitions of Awakened and Enlightened in mind, let's have a look at the teachers I discussed before. Firstly, what we can see is that in the process of becoming enlightened, during the awakening you often go through a phase of total enlightenment, where the ego completely falls away, and you are in a state of pure bliss. Osho, Eckhart Tolle and Mooji all went through this. Note that in this state it is very hard to function. When your ego completely drops away, it also means that any drive or ambition is gone. It is literally almost impossible to function in this world. Hence, Eckhart Tolle lived on a park bench for two years. Mooij was looked after by his sister. Osho was deemed going mad as he was just sitting doing nothing for a year.

I experienced this myself, after my first wave of awakening I was in such a state of emptiness, of no-mind, that my mind was so slow. Just to make a cup of tea was an effort and it took me ages. I could hardly talk with anybody. I just wanted to be alone, in silence.

What seems to happen is that after some time a little bit of ego comes back in, or perhaps it's more accurate to say that the person drops back down a bit into the awakened state. That is good in a way, as now you can function again in this society. Tolle and Mooji started teaching, Osho picked up his University studies.

So are these teachers Awakened or Enlightened? Let's look at them one by one.

Yogananda: as far as I can tell he managed to completely let go of sensuality and desires. I would say that he was enlightened to a very high degree. He was at peace, and he lived his life in service to bringing Kriya Yoga to the West.

Krishnamurti: He did let go of his sensuality (he hardly experienced this anyway) but with him there was a personality left, for example he was disappointed that no-one was able to follow him into the space he was in. But I would say that he was definitely enlightened.

Osho: Some people might be surprised when I say this about the "sex guru": but for me he was enlightened to a high degree. When you read his autobiography you can see that everything he was doing was to try to build a path for people to follow him into the state he was in. He was a true Zen Master, always confusing and surprising the students. For himself he didn't need anything. He was at peace.

Papaji: I have not studied him in-depth, but from watching several YouTube videos I would say he was enlightened.

Andrew Cohen: From his story it is clear that he definitely was awakened, but in time his ego came back. He dropped out of the awakened state. However I do have a lot of respect for him to admit this himself, and for offering an apology to his students.

Mooji: He is definitely awakened. I don't have enough information about him to come to a real conclusion, but it seems he is free of desires. I would say: enlightened.

Adyashanti: He seems to be very much at peace. However he did get married after his awakening. This to me shows that he is not free of sensuality and attachment. There is nothing wrong with that, but if you are truly enlightened you have no need for marriage. So in these terms he is awakened.

Eckhart Tolle: From what I can observe he came out of a very deep (and long) state of true enlightenment, but in time more and more ego returned. He also got married. They started building a whole marketing company around him. His photo's are being retouched. So my personal conclusion is: awakened.

Now you might think that I am being harsh and judgmental, or that I am against marriage. So let me be clear – I have no problem if Eckhart Tolle and Adyashanti got married (or anyone else for that matter). But for the purpose of understanding the difference between being Awakened and Enlightened it does make a difference. It does not mean that their teachings are not valid, in fact I have the deepest respect for the teachings of Adyashanti and Eckhart Tolle.

And what about myself I hear you ask? Yes, I had an awakening. I had a brief glimpse of what it means to be enlightened. But quite quickly my frequency dropped and my ego returned, and I have not gone beyond sensuality. Although my sense of mental peace has increased a lot, I would not say that I have gone into a state of permanent mental peace. Therefore I would not call myself Awakened (let alone Enlightened). But the whole experience did give me a deep understanding of how enlightenment works, both on a conscious level and on an energetic level. It is that insight that I want to share in this book.

How many people are enlightened?

This is hard to say. Estimates vary from 500 to 20,000 people (and I include the Awakened state in this). There are two main problems in answering this question. The first is that there is nobody who gives you a certificate when you get enlightened and put you on an official list!
Secondly: not everyone who becomes enlightened tells this to others. Osho only shared after 21 years that he had become enlightened. A lot of people never tell anyone.
Also: not every enlightened person becomes a spiritual teacher. Osho told a story of a man that he used to meet on a beach quite often. After some time he recognised that the man had become enlightened. But this man hardly ever spoke, all he did was make sand sculptures.

Are there any enlightened women?

It may seem from the people that I profiled that only men get enlightened. But luckily this is not the case. I chose the most well known masters, and for some reason they seem to be men. But there is a "new wave" of enlightened women coming onto the scene, some of them are:

Gangaji. She is an American woman and a disciple of Papaji. She is still human with sensuality.

Amma, the Indian "hugging Saint." She has an incredible compassion and unconditional love.

Yolande Duran is a French woman who became enlightened all of a sudden, without any suffering at all. She just dived into a deep state of inner stillness. So much so that even the death of her son two years later did not disturb her inner peace.

Dolano is a German woman, who has been living in Poona, India since 1979. She practiced excessive meditation and came to enlightenment after stays with Osho, Papaji and Gangaji.

Unmani is an English woman who spent most of her life living and travelling abroad. She stayed in the Osho ashram for some time and reached enlightenment after working with Dolano.

How do you reach enlightenment?

There are four main pathways to reach enlightenment:

1. Spontaneous awakening
This is rare, and by the fact that it is spontaneous it means that it is a path that one cannot copy. Eckhart Tolle and Jeff Foster are examples of this. Both were in great suffering when all of a sudden an insight happened and they had an awakening experience where the suffering ended. Yolande Durant became enlightened all of a sudden without any suffering at all. She just dived into a deep state of inner stillness.

2. Individual gradual awakening
Osho and Adyashanti are examples of this (though you might say that 14 years of Zen training helped Adyashanti move in the right direction). This path has not been charted very much, and this is the gap that this book hopes to fill.

3. Working with a Guru (Master)
This is the path of Yoga. What happens here is that somehow the energy flowing through the Guru manages to elevate the disciple to the same level and allows the awakening to happen. It is like the Guru is acting like a "cosmic tuning fork."
    - Andrew Cohen, Mooji and Gangaji all reached enlightenment after meeting Papaji.

- Papaji got enlightened during his stay with Maharishi.
- Yogananda achieved enlightenment with his Guru Sri Yuktsewar Giri.
- Several people have reached enlightenment after being with Osho, Dolani being the most well known.

4. Buddhism

Buddhism is arguably the only path that has found a consistent method to cultivate enlightened people. Examples are Thich Nhat Hanh, Dalai Lama, Dennis Genpo Merzel. However, not many people are prepared to spend years and years in deep Buddhist practise in order to get there.

Do you really want to become enlightened?

The idea of enlightenment may be attractive, and the promise of a "permanently peaceful mental state" sounds like a wonderful place to arrive at. But are you willing to go there? Are you really willing to do what it takes, and go through whatever is needed in order to get there? The problem with enlightenment is that no one can predict what kind of awakening experience you will have. Are you willing to lose your ego so much that you spend years hardly able to function in society? (Think of Osho, Eckhart Tolle, Mooji...) Are you willing to suffer years of intense physical pains? (Krishnamurti) Are you willing to undergo 14 years of deep Zen training like Adyashanti?

You could also argue that there is not much point in becoming totally enlightened. It is so difficult to function in the world in that state, that perhaps it is better to come back out of it and be in an Awakened state where you can function. However, this is what happens for most people anyway.

Maybe there is a way to "wake up" in such a way that you avoid the dramatic awakening process that is often experienced. This is what I am hoping to show you.

Did they manage to bring others to enlightenment?

Just because you are enlightened doesn't mean that you are able to bring others into that state as well. For example: Krishnamurti lamented at the end of his life that nobody had been able to follow him to the place where had arrived at. Eckhart Tolle is a great spiritual teacher, but I have not heard of people getting enlightened by following his teachings. The same counts for Mooji. You can watch and listen endlessly to video's from Tolle, Mooji, Adyashanti, but it won't mean that you will become enlightened. I will explain later why this is.

The teachers that have succeeded (Osho, Papaji, and a few others) only managed to lift a very few people into this state. So far only a very few people have been able to reach enlightenment. Is enlightenment possible for a large group of people? I will answer this question later...

Everybody is already enlightened

This is something that you hear a lot, especially by the Papaji / Mooji followers. But is it true? Just observe your own thoughts. Are you in a state of permanent peace? Yes, in our core essence we are all enlightened, we all have God inside us, but as long as you have not realised this and merged with this you are not enlightened.

Can anyone get enlightened in this life?

This is a very interesting question. There are roughly two schools of thought. The first one is that of the Advaita non-duality teaching of teachers like Papaji and Mooji. According to them anyone can reach enlightenment instantly, if they only realise their true essence. The second line of thought is the Buddhist view; that enlightenment is reached after many, many lifetimes, where one works to perfect oneself, and accrues merit in this life, in order to have a better reincarnation in the next life.

I think that both lines of thinking are right in a way. I agree that in principle it is possible to reach enlightenment if you truly realise your pure essence, your Self. But this is not as easy as it sounds, and only a very few people manage to have this kind of breakthrough. Why do certain people manage to get enlightened and the vast majority do not? Perhaps the Buddhists are right when they say that enlightenment only comes after many lifetimes of intense work, of trying to perfect yourself and taming the ego.

But there is something going on that has never happened before in the history of humanity. Something that might change everything. In the past, spiritual teachings were only available for a very select few people. Even in a deeply spiritual society such as Tibet, where it was normal that from almost every family one of the sons would go into a Buddhist monastery at a very young age, only a very few selected monks would get access to the full teachings.

But we now live in a time when information is openly available. Most people can follow the teachings of the Masters of our time on YouTube, and replay this over and over again if they want to. We live in a time where for millions of people the basic needs in life are met quite easily, and we have time and energy available to focus on spiritual development. I think that Osho was right when he said that "only from a position of wealth and comfort would the majority of people begin the return to God. When everything you've accumulated no longer makes you happy, you begin to ask the great questions. Who am I? Why am I here?"

If a normal person like myself is able to get an awakening experience, and a subsequently a change in consciousness like I have had, then surely this must be possible for many more people. I hope that the insights that I gained from this experience will help others to do the same. So who knows what will come out of all this?

Ascension and the 5th Dimension

As I am talking about enlightenment, I want to address the idea of ascension. There is a lot of talk these days in the "new age" community about the earth being in an "ascension process", where mankind is waking up, and we are supposedly all becoming enlightened and will move into the "5th dimension."

This idea of ascension to the 5th dimension is based on channellings of people with Ascended Masters. It's amazing how many people are able to communicate with the likes of Archangel Michael, Metatron, Kuthumi, Melchizedek etc! Now I am not disputing that it is possible to communicate with spirits (*after all I am communicating with my guides myself*), but one thing that I have learned over the years is that the information most people get via channelling is greatly influenced by their own belief systems. It is very, very hard to be a totally clear channel, and even then people only receive messages according to the level of consciousness that they are at *(and yes that counts for me as well)*. This actually makes perfect sense, because if you are only at level "ABC" and you would get messages talking about "XYZ", you wouldn't have a clue what they were talking about.

This whole idea of the ascension and the 5th dimension is just a belief system. Nobody really knows if it is true or not, and what does it mean anyway? Supposedly, when you are in the 4th dimension time does no longer exists. It is already incredibly hard to imagine what that is really like. The 5th dimension would go even beyond that, and our physical body would be a lot less dense. How can I understand the 5th dimension if I am already struggling to understand the 4th dimension?

Some people even claim that we have already moved into the 4th or 5th dimension, and that 5th dimensional consciousness is already here on earth. I find this hilarious. I don't know about you, but I am still experiencing time for example. It's all just a theory, a belief. All this talk about the 5th dimension has nothing to do with enlightenment. At best it is a complete form of spiritual flight. But a lot of the time these people are caught up in what I call "spiritual ego." Many teachers and channelers announced that on 21/12/2012 (end of the Mayan calendar), we would all ascend into the 5th dimension (end of the calendar, hence end of time, hence move to 5th dimension…) But guess what? It didn't happen. Since then I have seen several announcements (of course all received from the ascended masters, galactic councils, galactic federations and what have you not) that on such and such date the first wave of "lightworkers" would move into the 5th dimension and leave earth. Of course the people receiving these messages would be among first group of people to go. Well, they are still with us today.

One thing is interesting to observe: have you noticed that none of the enlightened masters ever talk about "the 5th dimension?" Why would that be, do you think?

Now I can hear you thinking: "but surely we are in an ascension process, people are waking up?" Maybe this is true, maybe it is not. Who knows? Around 1925-1930, Yogananda was speaking in front of thousands of people in the US. At the same time, Krishnamurti was speaking to audiences of 16,000 people. The Theosophical Society had 45,000 members. You might say that people were awakening. Then came the second world war.

You might say that now, with the help of the internet, more people than ever are waking up spiritually. In a way this is true, but tomorrow world war three may break out. Who knows? What I am saying is that the whole idea of ascension is a construction of the mind, of ego. We think that we know what is happening, but nobody really knows. It is all just a belief. And it does not matter.

The fact is that you and I came here to be on earth, at this time, in the 3rd dimension. And yes we are here to wake up. To remember who we really are, and to ultimately reach enlightenment. But there is no "easy exit" to the 5th dimension. No "energy wave" from the Universe will lift you into this state. Only you can do this yourself.

Part Two

The 5 principles of spiritual growth

13
The 5 principles of spiritual growth

In the awakening experience that I described in Part One I experienced two waves: the first wave was emptiness, the second was bliss.

I came out of this state quite quickly and returned to my "normal" ego state, but it allowed me to experience (for a brief time) what it is like to be enlightened and what happens energetically. I had a number of discussions with my guides to learn why it happened to me (as I wasn't actively looking for it) and more importantly how did I get to a state where this energy could come in?

What I learned is that in order to reach this state there are two main principles that apply: emptiness and bliss.

The emptiness refers to a number of elements: to empty yourself of stored emotions; to empty your mind. Bliss can be interpreted as raising your frequency. This can be done in a number of ways: physically, emotionally and mentally.

These two main principles can be broken down further into five principles. These are not just relevant if you want to reach enlightenment, they are the core principles that apply to the whole spiritual journey. They are:

1. Release your emotions
2. Raise your frequency
3. Heal your ego
4. Raise your consciousness
5. Connect to source

A crucial element is that you have to work on all of these levels. When combined, they create a synergy and you advance along the spiritual path much faster than when you work on just one of these areas. This is why watching YouTube video's from Mooji alone will not make you enlightened. It might temporarily bring you into a beautiful peaceful state, but if you are completely full of buried emotions, they will resurface and your ego will take over again.

You can use these principles as your compass that will help you on your spiritual journey. Whether your goal is to reach enlightenment, or "just" to experience more peace, happiness and health in your life, these five core principles remain the same.

In the next few chapters I will look at each of these principles in more detail, but what good is a compass if you don't have a map? So I will start by giving you that map, an overview of the Spiritual Journey of Life, the stages of spiritual development.

14
Stages of spiritual development

"We shall not cease from exploration. And the end of all our exploring will be to arrive where we started and know the place for the first time."
T.S. Eliot

This chapter gives an overview of the spiritual journey in life. All of life is spiritual, it's just that most of the time we are not aware of it.

To understand how life works, we need to go back right to the beginning, to the time we are born. We decided to come to earth and experience a new life on this beautiful planet.

Pure as a baby

A newborn baby is pure spirit in a tiny little fragile body. There is no mind yet, there is no ego, just pure being. This is why most people love babies. Think for a moment of the qualities that a baby has. You might say they are:

Pure, trusting, open, loving, fearless, unconditionally loving, direct, non-judgemental, innocent ...

If you met an adult who had all these qualities you would say this person is enlightened. So the irony is that we are born enlightened, only to lose it all. And then we spend our whole life trying to get back to this state.

So what happens? It is something that Don Miguel Ruiz (*from "The Four Agreements"*) calls "the domestication process." In psychological terms it is called "ego development." As the baby starts growing the brain function develops the capacity to think, and it starts to get domesticated. First the baby learns from its parents. It learns about judgment ("bad boy" or "good girl.") Then there are influences from family. When it becomes a toddler, the levels of influence increase. From friends of the parent, from other children, from the media, and all the time we tell the child what is "good" or "bad." When the child is "good" its gets a reward: love, attention, praise. When it is "bad" it gets punishment: it gets told off, left alone, toys get taken away, it might even get hit. The pure innocent child gets domesticated. We teach it how we want it to behave, how it should fit into this society.

The older the child gets, the more this happens. We tell it: "Boys don't cry", "man up", "don't be lazy", "you are so smart", "what beautiful clothes you are wearing", etc… Children need to behave, to "listen and do as I say" and do well at school, so they can get a good job later and be successful in life.

The first seven years of our life are the formative years when the personality is formed. It is also the time when we will experience our childhood traumas that will have a great effect on our life.

Roughly from the age of seven, influence from teachers come in. As teenagers, influences from peers play a large role. Doing well academically will play a major role now. Then they start work and get influenced by their boss and colleagues at work. The older we get, the more we are moulded to fit into society. We learn what is considered "right" or "wrong", what is "beautiful" and what is not, we learn the "rules of life", and all of this is according to the time and the society that we live in.

By the time you are a young adult (roughly 21 years old) you will have developed your mind and your personality, your ego. By now you will have completely identified yourself with your mind, with your personality. You belong to a nation, a race, a social class, a family, a university, a workplace, a sports team. The innocence is lost. You have become domesticated.

Osho had no conditioning. The first seven years of his life, the formative years, he was left mostly by himself. He remained free, he was not told what is good or bad, no rules of society were placed upon him. This allowed him to develop his own free thinking, his direct observation, his own judgment. By his own account this played a huge part in him becoming enlightened when he was twenty one years old.

By the time you are a young adult you are operating from mind, personality, from ego. Most of us were wounded during (early) childhood, and our ego is not whole, it is broken. We got wounded in love. Often we will have developed a victim mentality, where we feel that life is not fair and blame others for things that have happened to us. In doing so, we have given away our power. You operate mainly from your mind. And your mind operates on fear.

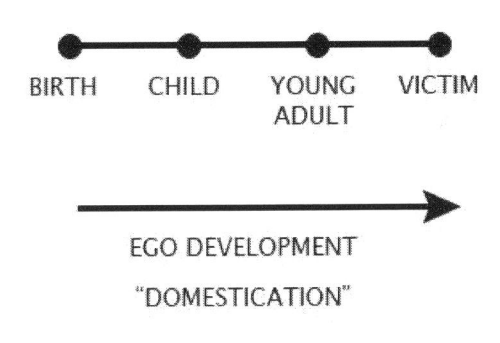

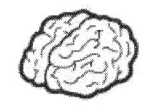

BIRTH — CHILD — YOUNG ADULT — VICTIM

⟶

EGO DEVELOPMENT

"DOMESTICATION"

MIND
EGO / PERSONALITY
FEAR

Waking up

So here you are, nicely conditioned. We learned the "rules of life", or rather how to operate in this society, but our soul does not care about these rules. Your soul does not care about material gain, about being successful at work, about having financial security. Your soul wants you to be free, to expand, to grow and develop into the most beautiful version of you.

So your soul starts stirring, and at some point you "wake up." For some people this is a gradual process, for others it really is a "wake up call", in the form of a spiritual crisis. This can be quite dramatic; an accident, a severe illness, loss of a relationship or job. Usually, your life gets shaken up in such a big way that you start to think about your life and re-evaluate what is important for you. You start to think about who you are and what you want out of life, why you are here. You have woken up from the dream.

The good news is that you have woken up already, otherwise you would not be reading this book right now!

In my case, the waking up process was very gradual and pleasant. It happened when I was twenty-six years old. My neighbour was talking about spirituality, and told me that I had spiritual talents too. I told her that I was not aware of anything. She said "Oh don't worry, when the time is right it will happen naturally." Then she told me about a book that had just been published that I might want to read: "*The Celestine Prophecy.*" I had never heard of it, I had never read a spiritual book. I was busy trying to "make it" in my IT career. I wrote down the name of the book and went home. The next morning the newspaper arrived, and in it was a big article with a review of "*The Celestine Prophecy.*" "That's a coincidence", I thought. After I read the paper (and the book review) I walked to the supermarket. On the way I passed a bookshop, and in a big window display was… yes you guessed it: "*The Celestine Prophecy.*" I was blown away. Less than 24 hours ago I had never heard of this book, now I came across it three times in a row. I bought the book. The first chapter talked about synchronicity and how signals often come in threes. I was amazed, and I was hooked.

At this point in time I was still living in Holland and was working for an IT company called "Logica." Not long after I had discovered *"The Celestine Prophecy"*, my team leader (and friend) at work had a dramatic spiritual awakening. Shortly after this he left the company, returned to London and became a Reiki Master. When I visited him he gave me a Reiki session one day. I will never forget it: as he put his hands on my stomach I could feel the energy flowing from his hands into my body. I felt like a battery being recharged. It was an incredible experience! When he told me that anyone can learn to do this, I decided to find a Reiki master in Holland and give it a try. At the end of 1996 I attended a Reiki 1 course. I loved it, and my spiritual journey became really conscious at this point.

Ownership

A crucial step in your development is when you stop being a victim and take ownership of your life. Of course this is not something you do overnight, it is a process that can take several years for some people. You will learn that you create your own reality (more on that in Part Four). Especially if your life is a bit of a mess it can be daunting to admit to yourself that you were the one who created it, but by taking ownership, you will reclaim your power and start to regain control over your own life. It is incredibly empowering.

When you have woken up spiritually and start to take ownership of your life, you will be able to consciously use the five principles that I am describing in this book. They will help you to make a lot of progress in a short space of time.

Mastery

The next stage in your development is Self-Mastery. This is about knowing who you are. This is where tools like NLP and The Law of Attraction come in. Where the goal of counselling and therapy is to heal people and to help them get from a broken ego to a healthy state, NLP (Neuro Linguistic Programming) looks at how successful people operate. It shows us how we can model their behaviour to go from a "normal" state, to becoming a master at what we do.

I love Mastery. I love it when people perfect their skill and reach the pinnacle of creation. Whether that is in music (Pink Floyd - The Wall, Michael Jackson - Thriller), art (Monet, Rembrandt), sports (the perfect 100m sprint, the football team that rises above themselves to win a match against the favourites). When people achieve a level that is special, it sends shivers down my spine.

But Mastery is about more than reaching the pinnacle of a career. It is about knowing yourself, knowing who you are, and who you are not. When you are an apple tree you need to know that you are an apple tree. There is no point trying to become a pear tree, even though all the people around you might be telling you that you should become a pear tree, that pears are what society wants. When you are an apple tree and you try to grow pears you will get a strange fruit. It won't work. The moment you realise that you are an apple tree and you stop trying to grow pears, you can relax. You can start to grow apples. You realise that you were always meant to be an apple tree. Your gift to the world is to grow apples. So your journey in life will be to become the best apple tree you can be, to grow the most beautiful apples.

We all have a gift to share with the world. Michael Jackson's gift was music. Lionel Messi's gift is football. Shakespeare's gift was prose. Rumi's gift was spiritual poetry, but a gift doesn't have to be something grand. Your gift may be to look after animals, or to produce wonderful bread for your community. No matter what your gift is, our job is to find it and share it with the world.

You will not reach Mastery when you are in a "victim consciousness", it just is not possible. Anyone who reaches a level of mastery has taken ownership of their life.

Reaching Mastery doesn't mean that you will be happy. Michael Jackson touched millions with his music, but he paid a heavy price in his personal life and was often deeply unhappy. In fact many artists seem to produce some of their best work when they suffer. When Pink Floyd recorded "The Wall" the tensions inside the band were terrible. Happy they were not, but they were at the height of their creative genius. I will talk more on happiness later in Part Four.

Spiritual Mastery

For some people, mastery turns out to be spiritual mastery. For them self-mastery literally becomes mastery of the Self.
In this case the next stages on the journey are Awakened and Full Enlightenment. I discussed this in detail in Part One, but will give a short summary here.

A person who is Awakened is free of identity view (ego) and attachments. There is still an ego, or I-identity, but they are no longer identified with the Ego. At this stage they still experience emotions, and still have (sensual) desires, but they are not ruled by their senses anymore. Most of the time they will be in a state of mental peace.

Being Enlightened is the ultimate state of spiritual development. In this state, all form of ego has gone, the ego (self) identity has completely dissolved, all (sensual) desires and any form of cravings have gone. You are in a state of great bliss and emptiness, you are in a permanent state of supreme mental peace. You are one with source.

Death

Each life starts at birth and ends with death. It is the final stage, and we all get there. Death is something we don't like to think or talk about. Deep inside we are afraid of it. So we choose to ignore it, as if by doing so it won't happen, but no-one can escape from it. It is never good to live in fear, and we can actually learn a lot from looking at death. I will discuss this in more detail later in Part Four. In order to make the "spiritual map" complete there is one thing I want to address:

Is there life after death?

This may be a difficult question to answer, at least from a scientific point of view. Science works by repeating an experiment, and if we get the same results each time then we can formulate a "scientific law" and declare certain "truths." The problem with death is that this is not an experiment you can repeat very easily!

Just because most people don't remember a previous life, this doesn't mean that we don't have any. But there are lots of people that do remember a previous life. There are very well documented cases that prove we have been here before.

One example is that of a four year old girl who went with her parents on holiday to France. When they drove through a little town the child saw a house and exclaimed "That's where I used to live!" She then described what the house looked like inside, what was in each room etc. In this case the parents went to the house, but the rooms were slightly different than the girl described. However, when they spoke to the owners they found out that 100 years ago the rooms were exactly laid out as the girl had described.

In his book, *"Children Who Have Lived Before: Reincarnation Today"*, German therapist Trutz Hardo shares extraordinary case studies of children from around the world who remember details of their past lives. One child in the Golan Heights, a region near the border of Syria and Israel, has an incredible tale:

A three-year-old of the Druze ethnic group, a group of people for whom reincarnation is a core belief, told his elders that he knew what had happened to him in his past life: he was murdered. The boy was born with a long, red birthmark on his head. For the Druse, birthmarks like these are an indication of death wounds, and children born with them are paid close attention to for anything they may remember of their past lives.

"As soon as a child is born its body is searched for birthmarks, since they are convinced that these stem from death wounds, which were received in a past life", Hardo writes. "If such marks are found on a child they try to discover something from his or her past life as soon as the child is able to speak in order to get the first clues to the circumstances of his or her former death."

Once this particular child turned three and could speak, he told his elders that he was killed by an axe blow to the head. He was led through villages to see if he could remember where he lived, until he came to one that seemed familiar to him. The child said he remembered both the first and last name of his killer with complete clarity. The boy confronted a man he'd never met but knowing his full name, claiming him to be the murderer.

"Suddenly the boy walked up to a man and said, "Aren't you so and so?" The man answered yes. Then the boy said, "I used to be your neighbour. We had a fight and you killed me with an axe." The man had suddenly gone white as a sheet. The three-year-old boy then said, "I even know where he buried my body."

Lo and behold, the boy led the elders to the exact spot, a pile of stones, under which there lay a buried body. The buried man's skull showed a split in the front. The boy also led the group to the spot where the axe was buried, forcing the accused killer to eventually confess his crime.

This is just one example, and there are lots of well documented cases like this. Buddhists, who have been studying consciousness for thousands of years, have mapped out life after death in great detail. For them, reincarnation is a normal accepted scientific fact, and for me it is the same.

Personally, I have memories of several past lives. In my previous life I was a fisherman in Greece, near Athens. I drowned in that life. It explains why I have a fear of drowning in this life (and I almost did, several times when I was young). It also explains why I get a deep, deep feeling of coming home when I step off the plane in Greece and smell the air.

People are often fascinated to find out about past lives, but not every past life is that of a high priest in Egypt! It can be very shocking to find out about your past lives, especially when you have acted in a way that is not in alignment with who you are today. This was true for me as well. For example in one past life I killed the woman that I was in love with in a blind rage, when she told me that she was in love with another man. In another life I left my pregnant wife and committed suicide. Of course you will have had wonderful lives too. A long time ago I was in a monastery in Tibet, though I was perhaps more fascinated with girls than with the endless meditations! But perhaps these are stories for another book...

Why do we forget all we have learned in past lives?

I often get asked this question: Why don't I remember anything when I am born? Why do I have to learn everything again that I have learned already in my past life? I need to learn to read and write again, learn maths, go to school...

Actually it is a real blessing that it works in this way. Can you imagine what it would be like to be in a little baby's body, but with a full consciousness as you have now? You can't speak, you can't walk, you are totally dependent on your parents. You want to be in the sun, but you can't speak. All you can do is cry. They take you to a busy cafe but the noise is too much for your sensitive ears. So you start to cry. And what is their response? They put a dummy in your mouth!

Yes it would be handy to remember how to read and write, but to come here with a full memory and fully conscious would be a torture in many ways. Instead, we are given a chance to "do it all over again." We get to experience the wonder of the first flowers in spring, the first snowflake on our hand and our tongue. We get to fall in love with life again.

In the afterlife (spiritual plane) we have full access to our life, and previous lives. Our awareness is on a much higher level. Then we come here and forget everything, so we can be pure.

THE SPIRITUAL JOURNEY OF LIFE

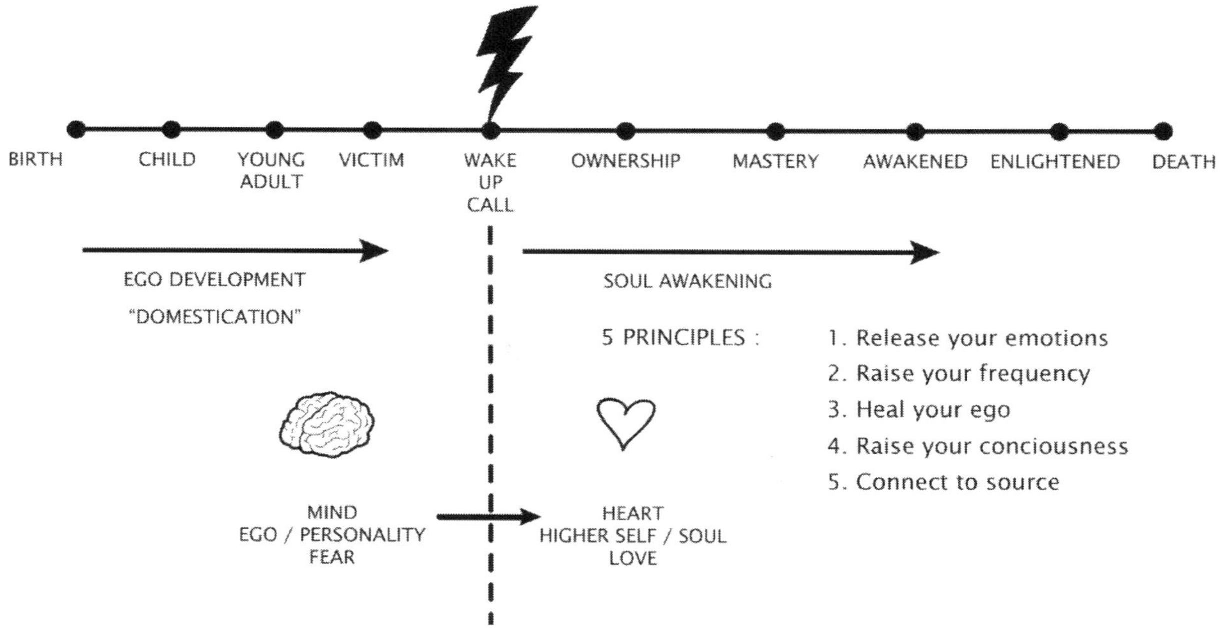

BIRTH — CHILD — YOUNG ADULT — VICTIM — WAKE UP CALL — OWNERSHIP — MASTERY — AWAKENED — ENLIGHTENED — DEATH

EGO DEVELOPMENT
"DOMESTICATION"

SOUL AWAKENING

5 PRINCIPLES :

1. Release your emotions
2. Raise your frequency
3. Heal your ego
4. Raise your conciousness
5. Connect to source

HEART
HIGHER SELF / SOUL
LOVE

MIND
EGO / PERSONALITY
FEAR

The spiritual transformation

In essence, the whole process of spiritual transformation after you wake up is about the following movements:

>   From mind to heart
>   From ego to soul
>   From fear to love

In order to progress from victimhood to ownership, from ownership to mastery, and from mastery to enlightenment you use the same five core principles:

1. Release your emotions
2. Raise your frequency
3. Heal your ego
4. Raise your consciousness
5. Connect to source

In the next few chapters I will describe each of these principles in more detail.

15
Releasing your emotions

The first of the five principles is to release your emotions. When you empty (release) your stored emotions, your will empty your mind. The correlation between the two might not be so obvious at first. So why is this so important you might ask? Let me explain.

The first thing to understand is the difference between your conscious mind and your subconscious mind. It is just like an iceberg – Our conscious mind is the tip above the water, maybe 10% or even less. The majority of mind activity is happening under the water in our subconscious mind.

Everything that happens in your life (*yes literally everything!*) is recorded in your subconscious. When you think of a memory, the information about a past event is brought from your subconscious to your conscious mind.

Now here is a question for you: Do you know what your next thought will be? Where does it come from? It seems like an impossible question to answer. Brain research has shown that our thoughts originate from our subconscious and "bubble up" to the surface and enter our conscious mind.

And we are always thinking of something! Our mind is constantly busy: observing what is happening, judging what is going on, going over the past, thinking of the future, it is never still. When you try to be still and meditate, thoughts keep coming in, bubbling up from your subconscious.

We can illustrate this process as follows:

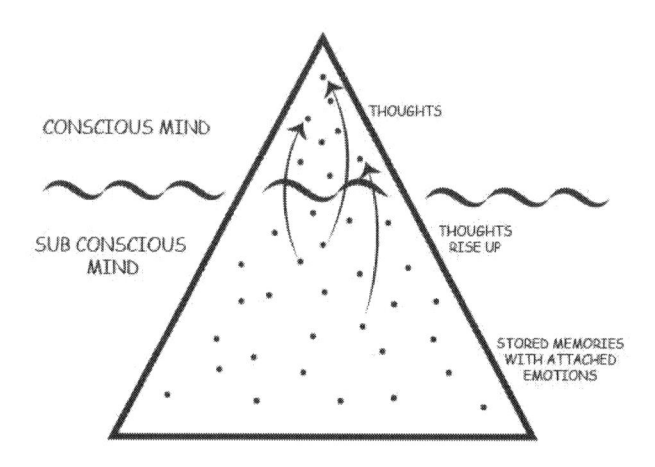

[Diagram: A triangle labeled with CONSCIOUS MIND at the top above a wavy line, and SUB CONSCIOUS MIND below. Arrows show THOUGHTS RISE UP from STORED MEMORIES WITH ATTACHED EMOTIONS to become THOUGHTS.]

But this picture is not complete yet, something else is happening too. At all times your Soul is trying to come through to you. Your soul energy is literally entering your crown chakra and trying to fill you up with more of your Self.

The problem is that you are so full of mind activity that you can't hear your soul, you can't feel it. You are literally so full of mental energy that the soul energy can't come through very much. It is a bit like the weather. Your soul is like the sun. It is always shining. Our mind is like the clouds. If our mind is clouded we cannot see the sun.

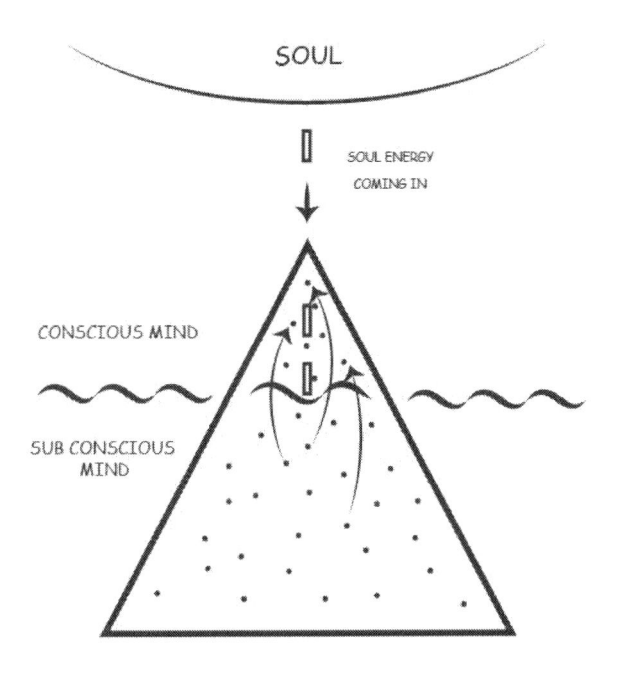

So when you empty your mind, your soul energy can come through more, and your frequency goes up. So here is how enlightenment works: at some point when you have emptied yourself to a certain point, the soul energy comes rushing in and washes you clean. It is a bit like a dam that a beaver has built; when you keep removing the sticks one by one, at some point it will get so weakened that it will burst and the water comes rushing in. The same happens with you. Literally the more empty you become, the better you will feel and the closer you will get to enlightenment.

A key to let go of your thoughts is to let go of your stored emotions. Emotions function like an anchor, keeping hold of the memories (thoughts). You can observe this for yourself. The events that you can remember from your childhood are the situations that have a high emotional charge. These can be "good" or "bad" memories, the principle is the same. Every day events that have no real emotional charge you will have forgotten, which only means that they do not surface to your conscious mind so easily.

When you let go of the emotional charge of past events, these memories will not surface to your mind anymore. You will become more empty, more at peace.

There are various techniques to let go of emotions; Tapping (EFT), Healing codes, Emotion Code, Ho'oponopono, and others. I will discuss this in much more detail in Part Three.

When I asked my guides which practices had been the most influential in leading me to my awakening experience, they told me that from all the things that I had done two things stood out: one was clearing my emotions, the second was the MerKaBa meditation. I will tell more about the MerKaBa meditation later.

As for clearing emotions: I did a lot, and I mean really a lot. Most clients that come to me with an issue will work on clearing the emotions that are at the root of the problem. Once the problem has been resolved the client stops. I did not stop. I made extensive lists of every major event in my life that I could think of, and bit by bit cleared all these emotions. I just wanted to become as empty, as clear as possible (*and not with the motivation to get enlightened, I did not think about that at all at the time*).

16
Raising your frequency

*"If you want to find the secrets of the universe,
think in terms of energy, frequency and vibration."*
Nikola Tesla

*"What we have called matter is energy, whose vibration has been
so lowered as to be perceptible to the senses. There is no matter."*
Albert Einstein

The second principle is: raising your frequency. In this chapter I will explain what I mean by this and why this is so important.

Everything has a frequency

We are pure energy. We think that we have a solid body, but when you "zoom in", all you will see is a lot of space with some molecules. If you "zoom in" on the molecules, you will see 99% empty space with some atoms. Atoms are 99.9% space with electrons and protons spinning around at a certain velocity. Your body is literally vibrating at a certain frequency.

Everything has a particular frequency. Your thoughts have a certain frequency. Science can actually measure the frequency of thought waves. Different thoughts have a different frequency. Your emotions have a certain frequency. It will come as no surprise that love has a higher frequency than fear.

Perhaps this whole concept has been illustrated the best by the late Dr. Masaru Emoto. He conducted experiments where he froze water molecules and took pictures under a microscope, to show the effect that sound, emotions and thoughts have on water.

The images above are from frozen water molecules, taken by Dr Masaru Emoto. On the left water was exposed to the words "Love" and "I will kill you." On the right is water taken from the Fujiwara dam. This water was badly contaminated (top picture). A group of people came around the lake and sent prayers to the water. The effect can be seen in the bottom picture.

When you realise that your body is made up of around 70% water, you can start to imagine the impact that your thoughts and emotions have on your body.

Every expression through sound, emotion, or thought, holds a specific frequency which influences everything around it, much like a single drop of water can create a large ripple effect in a body of water.

There is another famous experiment that illustrates the power of thoughts and words perfectly. This is the plant experiment, where one plant is told "I love you", another plant is ignored, and the third one is told "I hate you." The next pictures will show the effect:

Start

One month later

As you can see, surprisingly getting no attention at all is even worse than being told "I hate you." Apparently any attention is better than no attention, which explains perhaps on one level why people stay in abusive relationships.

Our goal is to raise our frequency. On one level you might say that perhaps this is the whole purpose of our life.

The higher your frequency becomes, the smaller gap there is between your pure state (soul state) and your "normal" state. Hence you will experience a less dramatic awakening experience.

Spiralling up, spiralling down

Our frequency is always changing, it never stays at the same level for long. It tends to either go up, or go down. This does not tend to be a linear process, it might be better to think of it as spiralling up and spiralling down. Hence the expressions: "he is spiralling down", or: "the situation is spiralling out of control." The key is to become aware at all times where you are: is your frequency going up or down at this moment?

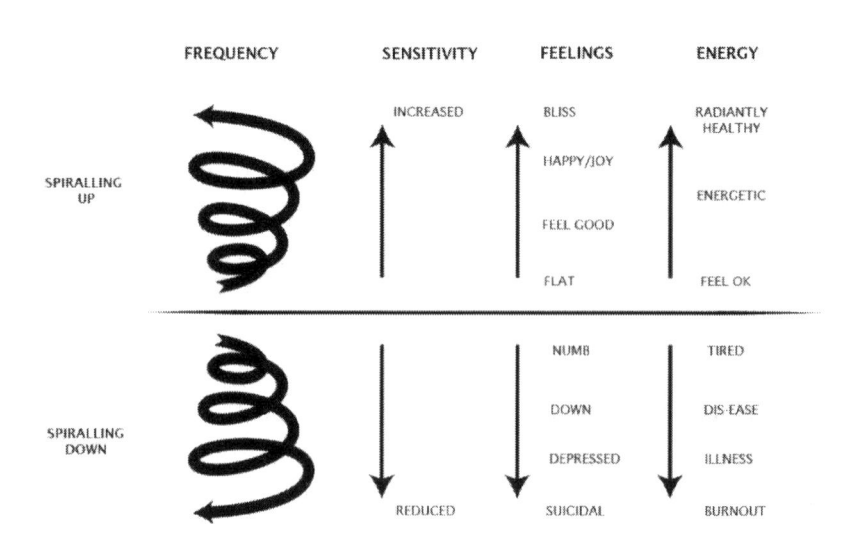

	FREQUENCY	SENSITIVITY	FEELINGS	ENERGY
SPIRALLING UP		INCREASED	BLISS HAPPY/JOY FEEL GOOD FLAT	RADIANTLY HEALTHY ENERGETIC FEEL OK
SPIRALLING DOWN		REDUCED	NUMB DOWN DEPRESSED SUICIDAL	TIRED DIS-EASE ILLNESS BURNOUT

There is one thing that is absolutely crucial to become aware of: the turning point. This is the point where you are on the threshold. At this point you can go either up or down. When you get below this threshold, you start to spiral down and it gets really hard to reverse this. Initially it is still possible, but when you go too low your energy levels go down so much that it gets harder and harder to stop the fall. When this happens, people often need to hit rock bottom before they can turn the situation around.

It is important to remain above this threshold at all times, so you need to learn to recognise where that threshold is for you. This is very individual, it is different for every person. So how can you recognise where that threshold is? You can find this out by observing your feelings and energy levels.

When your frequency goes up, your emotional state improves, from feeling flat to: feeling good, experiencing joy, happiness, and ultimately a state of bliss. Below the threshold, when your frequency goes down, you start to feel numb, feel down, you go into depression, and ultimately you end up feeling suicidal.

When your frequency goes up you will get more energy. You will start to feel better, more energetic, resulting in radiant health and an abundance of energy. When your frequency goes below the threshold, you start to feel tired. If it goes down further you will experience dis-ease, resulting in illness and ultimately a burnout.

When your frequency goes up your sensitivity increases (and vice versa). This explains why "normal" people can eat pizza, drink beer and they seem to be totally fine (at least on the surface). The higher your frequency gets, the lighter you (and your body) become, the less tolerant your system will be for this kind of food and lifestyle. What is really happening is that you are becoming more sensitive and you are beginning to hear the feedback signals that your system is giving you, about what is good for it and what is not.

To recognise this process of frequency going up or down within yourself, and to ensure that you keep above the threshold, is a fundamental tool that will help you progress on your spiritual journey.

High frequency living

So what can you do to raise your frequency? Actually there are lots of things you can do! Here is a list that we put together on one of my workshops:

Healing
Meditation
Going to high energy places
Listen to music
Dancing
Meet up with positive friends
Walk in nature (beach, woods, mountains...)
Spending time by yourself
Gardening
Art
Yoga
Watch an inspiring movie
Read a good book
Doing sports (gym, running, swimming...)
Connecting with Sacred Geometry
Create a beautiful space (crystals, mandalas, candles, flowers...)
Have a bath with essential oils
The list really is endless, and it is very individual.

Now let's have a look at all the spiritual practices and self-development methods, and how they fit in. Below is a list of the most popular practices. It is by no means a complete list, but you will get the idea:

Physical	Emotional	Mental	Spiritual
Food Sport Dancing Yoga Reiki	Music Kirtan (chanting) EFT Ho'oponopono Healing code Emotion code	NLP Gratefulness Affirmations The Secret The Journey Counselling Satsang	Gong Bath Mindfulness Meditation MerKaBa

As you can see, I have divided this into four categories:
Physical / Emotional / Mental / Spiritual.

Some practices work mainly on the physical level (sport), some others on the mental level (affirmations), but everything is linked. For example, when you feel better physically your emotional state improves as well. When you feel better emotionally your mental state improves too.

For example, food has a direct impact on your emotional and mental states (more on that later), as do sports. It is hard to meditate (spiritual) when you are exhausted physically. When you heal your emotions, your physical health improves. Actually most, if not all, physical problems have an emotional cause. I will share a lot more on that in Part Three.

So the art of "super high frequency living" is to apply ALL of this to your life! Of course you cannot do all of this is one week or one month. This is why it often takes years to really move ahead on the "spiritual ladder." But any of these methods will raise your frequency, so find what resonates for you and do it!

How to bring your frequency down

Just as it is important to know how to raise your frequency, it is also important to know what brings your frequency down. Again, this is individual, but here are some things that get mentioned a lot in my workshops. I divided them into categories:

Physical: too much food, "heavy" food, alcohol, not enough sleep, spending time on screens (computer, TV, phone).

Emotional: being a victim, anger, fear.

Mental: being in an ego state, worry, stress, spending time with negative people.

Spiritual: disconnected from soul/source, not aligned with purpose, spiritual pride.

So here the solution is simple: stop doing these things, or at least minimise them!

Keeping the fire burning

A lot of "spiritual" people are empaths: they feel others and often use a lot of their energy in helping others. They are givers. It is especially important for these people (but really for all of us) to keep their energy levels up, to keep their fire burning. Probably the fastest way to lower your frequency is by depleting yourself.

So what keeps your fire burning? What gives you energy? It is super important to realise this for yourself. For example, what really works for me is: music, dancing, walking on the beach, seeing the joy of my dog on the beach, hugs, meeting up with positive friends… When I feel low then music, dancing and walking on the beach are great ways for me to lift my frequency and energy levels. Then I can go and meditate to connect more. However, if I feel low meditation will not work initially. I first need to be "high enough" for it to lift me up further. But this it is how it is for me, for you it might be different. It is important to find out what works for you.

Exercise:

Start by writing down all the things you love doing. Don't think too much about it, just write them down and think of the next thing.

Once you have written down the obvious things that you are aware of, look back at your life. What have been the highlights of your life? What did you love? When did you feel really good? Write this down too.

Then think of your childhood. What did you love to do then? Sometimes we have forgotten how to play and have forgotten the things we loved as a child. Again, write this down.

> Look at all the things you have written. You may start to see some themes there – for example some activities might be connected with nature, or with sports, or with music.
> You might have re-discovered some activities that you have not done for a while, or that you always wanted to do but never had the opportunity to.
>
> Look again at your list. Select those things that will lift you up when your frequency and energy levels go down. Write this down. This is your "frequency booster plan." There is no use in just writing this down, you have to do it! *Especially* when you feel flat and can't motivate yourself to do anything.

Food and Drinks

There is one area that I want to focus on a bit more before I move on to the second of the five principles: food & drinks. What we eat and drink has a direct impact on our frequency.

I have said before that our body is 70% water. Dr Emoto has shown what effect thoughts and emotions have on water. So what you drink makes a huge difference to your frequency. If you want to raise your frequency you can do the following:

- Stop drinking alcohol (which numbs your senses and lowers your frequency)
- Stop drinking milk (which is mucus forming)
- Don't take any fizzy drinks (lots of sugar, or even worse sugar replacements like aspartame that may damage your brain)

Instead, drink a lot of water and herbal teas. Coffee is ok, but in moderation (as it is very acidic). Try to limit it to one cup per day.

Blue Solar Water

Something that I have learned from Dr. Huh Len (*the man who made Ho'oponopono famous in the west, more on that in Part*

Three) is Blue Solar Water.

To make Blue Solar Water you put normal tap water in a blue bottle and put this in sunlight. It does not have to be directly in the sun but that does work better. After an hour the water is cleansed and charged up, by a combination of the sun with the blue bottle. It makes the water taste much softer and just delicious. My body can feel the difference!

I often do a blind test with visitors, and everybody is amazed at the difference. They can't believe that the water came from the tap. A friend of mine is very good with plants, but once she had a plant that was not doing well, no matter what she tried. Then she started giving it Blue Solar Water (with no other changes) and within a week it was flourishing!

So if this water has such a direct effect on that plant, can you imagine what it will do for your body? I produce all my drinking water in this way. I put the blue bottle on an image of the Flower of Life (sacred geometry) and put a sacred geometry crystal on top of the bottle (*I use the star tetrahedron for this , I will describe this later when I talk about connecting to source*). This way the water becomes super charged. I can feel it when I drink it! Try it for yourself.

Food

I could write a whole book about food (which I am not planning to do). But as I am discussing high frequency living, I do want to mention a few things about food. I must admit that for years I was completely confused about food. There are so many different diets, so many contradicting opinions, every week you hear about a new "superfood" – What is true and what is not?

The book *"The Food Hourglass"* changed all that for me. It is written by Dr Kris Verburgh, a Belgium journalist and doctor, who did a lot of research on all the research on food. I cannot recommend this book highly enough. Apart from explaining why certain foods are good or not good for you, he introduces the idea of slowly swapping "bad" foods with "good" foods. This way you don't have to go on a diet, but as you swap more unhealthy foods for better options, bit by bit your diet improves. Some simple rules that you can follow are below:

- Cut out white pasta, white rice, bread and sugar from your diet as much as possible. Replace this with rye bread, oats, brown rice, millet, quinoa.

- The amount of vegetables on your plate should be double the amount of your pasta, rice or potatoes (not the other way around, like most of us normally have).

- The evening meal should be your smallest meal. If you eat less in the evening you will sleep better. And don't snack just before you go to bed, your body should be doing a "mini fast" at night and recharge itself, not using energy to process the food that you ate at 11pm.

- In general, we eat too much: all research confirms that in order to live longer you should eat less. What happens is that your body uses more energy to process all the (heavy) food it gets, than it gets from the food. This explains that when you eat less you need less sleep.

- Often when you feel hungry, what your body really needs is more water. We usually don't drink enough. Drinking 6 to 8 glasses of water a day will keep your body hydrated and will help to release toxins from your body.

"What about meat?" I hear you ask. Well, the way I think about meat is this: There is no "medical" reason why we should eat meat. You can easily meet all your nutritional needs with a vegetarian diet. So we are killing and eating animals just because we like the taste of them. I love animals, why should I kill and eat what I love? Secondly, for me it is completely obvious that all the fear and the stress that the animal experiences just before it gets slaughtered goes into the meat, no matter what a good life that animal may have had. You are literally eating the animal's stress and fear. This is obviously not going to raise your frequency. I am not saying that you can't be spiritual if you eat meat, and I feel that everybody needs to make their own decision on this, but for me it is inevitable that if you really want to raise your frequency you will stop eating meat.

You are what you eat. If you eat lighter food, you will literally become lighter. You might lose weight (though that is not my goal here at all), but most of all you will feel better, you will have more energy, your health will improve, you will live longer. Your frequency goes up!

17
Healing your ego

"We all got wounded in love"
Roberto Assagioli

"You cannot fly with broken wings"
Unknown

One of the biggest fallacies in spiritual teachings is that we should let go of our ego. You hear this over and over again, but the truth is that we need an ego in order to function in the world. When I had my awakening experience, my ego fell away completely for a short while and I could hardly function at all. Even making a cup of tea was a struggle and I became sooo slow at doing things!

Eckhart Tolle spent two years on a park bench after he became enlightened and was without ego. So unless you want to spend the rest of your life on a park bench, I would suggest you keep your ego.

Maybe it is a good idea to explain what I mean when I use the word "ego", as the term is used in different ways. When I talk about ego I talk about your personality, or your adaptive self. It is the personality that you have developed since you were born. Another way to put this is to say that your ego is your mind identification, all the thoughts that you have formed about yourself.

When your ego (your personality) is broken, it is very hard to go into a state of enlightenment (no ego or small ego). Yes it can happen, and a few people, like Eckhart Tolle, or Jeff Foster, did go from a state of deep suffering directly to a state of enlightenment. But this is very rare.

The path with a much better chance of real and lasting progress, is to heal your ego, to heal your wounding from childhood. Before you can let go of your ego, you need to make it stronger, make it healthy. It is much easier to let go of your personality from a place of healthy self esteem and self love, than from a place of low self esteem and self hatred.

This principle explains why there is a limitation to listening to teachers like Mooji and Adyashanti. Yes, their teaching is valid, and yes, it might temporarily lift you into a state of higher consciousness (especially in a satsang where there is a direct energy transfer from the teacher to the student), but inevitably you come back down again and your (broken) ego comes back in. It is very hard to let go of a broken ego.

You cannot fly with broken wings. So if your ego is broken – heal it! This principle is illustrated graphically below. If you could see the energy of the body, of the mind, and the aura - then this is what you would see:

Broken ego	Healthy ego	Small ego
Obsessive mind activity	Active mind	Mind is still
Emotional wounds	Usual emotions	Emptiness
Pain, Fear	Conditional love	Unconditional love
Anger, Blaming	Judgement	Compassion
Worry	Joy	Bliss
Low frequency	Normal frequency	High frequency

When you look at energy this way it becomes totally obvious that in order to get to the enlightened state you first need to heal, in order to let go.

Most people on the spiritual path would benefit more from therapy and other forms of self-healing than going on a workshop to connect with the angels. I would go as far as saying that this applies to 95% of "spiritual seekers."

How can you heal the ego?

The most effective way to heal your ego is to combine working on an emotional level with that on a mental level. This will generate a synergetic effect where these two approaches will enhance each other.

It is great if you work on releasing stored emotions, but that alone is not enough. You need to heal the personality too. You need to heal your limiting beliefs. You need to get a healthy self esteem, to stop being a victim and take ownership for your own life. All this is needed order to make your ego (personality) whole again.

Some techniques that work at an emotional level are: EFT, Ho'oponopono, Healing code, Emotion Code.

Some techniques that work on a mental level are: NLP, Affirmations, The Journey, Counselling, Psychotherapy.

It is beyond the scope of this book to discuss the process of healing the ego in detail, but I will discuss Emotions in Part Three, and the Mind in Part Four.

18
Raising your Consciousness

"The whole effort of a Jesus or a Buddha is nothing but how to undo that which society has done to you"
Osho

I have talked about raising your frequency, releasing your emotions and healing your ego. Another key principle is to raise your consciousness. What I mean by that is to become more aware of your life, and of life in general. This is about waking up from the dream, and undoing the conditioning. To becoming aware of how you are functioning in an ego state, how you are trapped in your mind all the time. It is about learning to tame your mind, to free yourself and become aware of the Self. It is unlikely that you will reach enlightenment doing a nine to five job, reading the tabloids, following Kim Kardashian on Instagram, watching soaps on TV in the evening, eating pizza and drinking beer. I'm not saying that it's impossible, but somehow I doubt it.

Sometimes becoming more conscious can be thrilling and exciting. For example when I learned Reiki and discovered how energy works I was so excited! It was wonderful to discover these capabilities in me, and to find out that there is so much more to life than I knew before. The same counts for discovering the "law of attraction": it is thrilling to get a better understanding of how we create our reality, and the increased power that it gives us to shape the life in the way we want. It empowers us to become a co-creator.

At other times, becoming more conscious can be very challenging. Sometimes you will look at old belief systems and have to admit that things are maybe not as you thought they were. No-one likes to be "wrong", and you might feel a resistance to change the way you view the world and view life.

For example, when I learned about the Illuminati *(the people who control the society)*, and how they control and manipulate people in order to stay in power, I had a huge reaction. I got angry, I did not want this to be true. Surely the world could not be such a bad place? Surely the government in Holland would not take part in this? (*I had always felt proud of Holland being such an open and tolerant country.*) It took me some time to come to terms with this, but eventually I had to look at the evidence and admit to myself that my old view was not correct, or at least was incomplete.

The difficult part of raising your consciousness is that as you become more aware, you will be forced to makes changes in your life. And most people resist change.

I remember when I was a teenager I used to go fishing with my parents. I loved carp fishing. I totally loved carps, I thought they were beautiful, they had such a power and were so smart. When I managed to get one on the line it was not just a matter of reeling it in, this was really a fight to see who was the strongest and the smartest. If I gave it a bit too much room it would do a few circles through the reed beds and there would be no way I could get it in, the line would break. If I caught one and it was bleeding from the hook I would find it terrible, I really did not want the carp to hurt. Slowly I started to think about what I was doing. I realised that if I really loved these fish, I should not be catching them. So I stopped fishing. That is what raising consciousness is about.

One of my pet "hates" at the moment is air shows. Where I live in England at the moment there is a yearly air show of the Red Arrows and other war planes. Hundreds of thousands of people come to Bournemouth each summer to watch the display of these planes. Lots of my spiritual friends post excitedly on Facebook about it. But to me it doesn't make sense. We are against war. We don't want our government to bomb Syria. But we celebrate the glory, the speed and the power of these planes? These are war machines. They were designed and built to do combat in the air, to drop bombs on people. And here we all are, on the beach, cheering as they fly over us at great speed.

In a way it is easier to stay asleep, so you can enjoy your pizza, drink your beer, read your tabloid and enjoy the air show. But you have woken up. Your soul inside you is stirring. It wants you to learn. It wants you to grow. It wants you to be the best version of yourself that you can be.

Krishnamurti's teaching was completely focussed on raising your consciousness. What he wanted to do was to make you think, to really examine all aspects of your life. He was razor sharp. Initially when I was reading his book "Freedom from the known" I could not read more than two pages at a time. It's not a very thick book, about 150 pages, but it took me forever to get through it. After reading two pages I would have to re-read it and think about what he was saying. This book is so full and so sharp. It had a major impact on some people, because it challenged their whole belief system.

You may ask at this point: "why it is so important to become more conscious?" The short answer is that it is about undoing the conditioning, about seeing reality. Ultimately when you realise what you really are, when you realise your Self, you will be free. You have become Self-Realised. This is what the whole teaching of Papaji, Mooji, Adyashanti and others is about.

Raising your consciousness is such a large subject and it so important, that I will dedicate Part Four of this book to it. I will discuss topics such as: how your mind is a filter, how you create your reality, karma, fate and destiny, what is love and fear, how mind equals fear, the difference between problems and luxury problems, and the existential questions: Who am I? Why am I here? What is my life all about? I will show you how you can free yourself of your mind, and connect to your soul.

19
Connecting to source

"Darkness is an absence of light. Ego is an absence of awareness"
Osho

"Quiet the mind and the soul will speak"
Ma Jaya Sati Bhagavati

When we connect to source, we connect to something that is much bigger than us. We connect to nature, to life, to the force behind everything, to that which controls and gives life to the whole universe. This has been given different names: "Universe", "God", "Tao" or whatever you want to call it. The importance is not to get hang up on names or definitions. It is about getting a direct experience yourself.

When you connect to source it means you automatically connect to your soul. More of your soul energy can come in. Your frequency will go up. Your mind becomes more silent. You will start to feel joy for no apparent reason, just for witnessing the incredible beauty that is your life, that is life on this planet. You will connect with unconditional love.

Ultimately enlightenment happens when your soul energy completely fills you up. This is why all the masters tell us time and time again that we should meditate. Meditation is the direct path to your soul. You empty your mind and connect to source, to your soul. The Buddha reached enlightenment after a period of intense meditation. Osho spent a year completely in meditation before he reached enlightenment.

But there are different ways to connect to source, not just meditation. I will discuss some paths below, before sharing a bit more about meditation.

Stillness

When you go into stillness, when your mind goes silent, you will connect with source. When this happens, you create the space for your soul energy to come in and fill you up.
To experience stillness, you don't have to sit down on a cushion and meditate. There are different ways how you can get into a quiet still space. Gazing into a fire is one good way. Fishing is another: when you are staring for hours at the float, to see if it goes under, at some point your mind goes still. I have experienced the same effect when I was sailing: after hours and hours of steering the boat, looking at the waves and the sails, being at sea with no other distractions around, I sometimes entered into this deep stillness, being one with the boat and the sea.
These are just a few examples, but you will get the idea. There are numerous ways in how you can achieve this state. What works for you? When and how do you enter into stillness?

Connecting to nature

One very powerful way to connect to source is to connect with nature. When you go for a walk in nature, and you really connect with the beauty and the perfection of nature, it will totally connect you to source. What is important here is not to go into your mind and go like "Oh this is a mulberry bush, and there is a beautiful old oak tree." Try not to label what you are seeing, but to get a direct experience of it, just observing, immersing yourself in the experience.

Paradoxically enough, taking photographs in nature can sometimes connect me much deeper. Somehow when I am looking to find an interesting and beautiful picture, it makes me look in a different way. Just a single leaf, or a pebble on the beach, the way the light shines, can take me into such a state of beauty that my heart chakra completely opens up and I get lifted into a total state of love, feeling completely connected to all life, to source.

Running

"Running?" You might ask. Yes, really. People who run will know what I am talking about. When you go running, sometimes you will experience what is known as the "runners high." At a certain point, when have been going for a while, you are tired and your legs are aching, when all suddenly all the pain goes and it is like you are flying along without any effort at all. You feel fantastic, sometimes even euphoric. On a physical level the effect is produced by the release of endorphins by your body, but on a spiritual level when this happens you are connected to source, your mind is still, and you are totally alive.

A similar effect can happen with other activities as well, dancing for example. The combination of the music, together with moving your body, can take you in a heightened state where you disappear, your mind goes silent, and you go into a state of bliss.

Intense action sports

A similar effect (though in a very different way) happens when you perform intense action sports. It can be car racing, big wave surfing, skiing, or rock climbing for example. It applies to any sport where you have to be totally concentrated, or you might seriously injure yourself (or even lose your life). You have to concentrate so intensely that you will have no time to think. You will be so completely in the moment, in the now, that you disappear. Your mind is silent, yet you are totally alive, totally present in the moment. You are completely connected.

Sex

Some people will be horrified that I put Sex in here, but the truth is that Sex can be a very powerful way to connect to source. When you are intensely connected to the other person and you experience an orgasm, it can happen that for a very brief moment your mind completely fall away, and you merge with source, you experience the oneness, a total state of bliss.

In fact, for many people this will be the only time in their life that they will experience this state of oneness, of bliss. This is one of the reasons why people get addicted to sex, they want to repeat this experience, to hold on to it. But of course this is not possible, and after the peak experience of orgasm there is the comedown, the tiredness or even exhaustion after having sex.

Meditation

I am not proposing that you start running, go car racing and engage in lots of sex in order to connect to source. I have included these activities here in order to give a full overview of the different ways that people can have an experience of connection to source. Stillness and Connecting to Nature are ways that bring a different quality of connection, and come much closer to the ultimate form of connecting to source: meditation. There are numerous ways how to meditate, below I will give a brief overview of some of the most common techniques.

Mindfulness

This meditation technique has its origin in Zen Buddhism, and has become incredibly popular in the last few years. It is in essence a practise of awareness. You start with bringing your awareness to your breath. Later this is expanded to becoming aware of your thoughts, feelings and actions. A famous exercise is that in which a raisin is being tasted and eaten mindfully. You might even say that the activities of Stillness and Connecting to nature, that I described earlier, are a form of mindfulness.

Transcendental Meditation (TM)

This is a meditation technique that was developed by Maharishi (*he was the enlightened Indian guru that The Beatles followed for some time*). In TM you receive a personal word (mantra), and focus your mind completely on this. Anytime a thought comes in, you remember the mantra and focus on this. Eventually you mind will go more and more silent.

TM gained a lot of attention after experiments were conducted where one thousand trained TM meditators came together in Washington to meditate three times a day. As they had predicted, the result of generating a strong energy field of peace and love was that violence and crime rates in the city dropped. This experiment has been repeated and validated through scientific studies various times, and is called the "Maharishi effect."

In the second phase of TM students ago into such a deep meditative state that they may experience a form of levitation – this is called "Yogic flying." I must say that I don't understand how this works, but it is just because I don't understand something does not mean that it is not real. It seems that there really are no limits to what we can do.

Dynamic Meditation

This meditation technique was developed by Osho after he realised that Western people had great difficulty in meditating, as their mind would just not be still. It has four stages, each lasting ten minutes.

In the first stage you stand with your eyes closed and breathe deep and fast through your nose for ten minutes. You allow your body to move freely. You jump, sway back and forth, or use any physical motion that helps you pump more oxygen into your lungs.

The second stage is one of catharsis. You let go totally and be spontaneous. You may dance or roll on the ground. Screaming is allowed and encouraged. You must act out any anger you feel in a safe way, such as beating the earth with your hands. All the suppressed emotions from your subconscious mind are to be released.

In the third stage you jump up and down yelling "Hoo! Hoo! Hoo!" continuously for ten minutes. This sounds silly, but the loud vibration of your voice travels down to your centres of stored energy and pushes that energy upward. When doing this stage, it is important to keep your arms loose and in a natural position. Do not hold your arms over your head, as that position can be medically dangerous.

The fourth ten minute stage is of complete relaxation and quiet. You flop down on your back, get comfortable and just let go. Be as a dead man totally surrendered to the cosmos. Enjoy the tremendous energy you have unleashed in the first three stages and become a silent witness to the drop as it flows into the ocean. Become the ocean.

MerKaBa Meditation

This meditation technique was developed by a man called Drunvalo Melchizedek. It is less well known, but extremely powerful, in fact this meditation is a complete energy workout.

It consists of 17 specific breaths that combine mudras (hand positions), a specific focus on the breath and visualisations based on sacred geometry. It has three phases.

In phase one you cleanse and balance the electromagnetic circuits and chakras in your body.

In phase two you work with Prana breathing (*Prana is life force energy*) to create a very strong energy field around you. You will move the centre of your energy from the 3rd chakra to your heart chakra. This is very significant, as you move from your power centre (ego) to your heart: unconditional love.

In phase three you create a flying saucer shaped energy field around you, this is called the MerKaBa. This field is very large (55ft wide) and incredibly powerful.

The MerKaBa meditation cleanses and strengthens your energy field, raises your frequency, and connects you to source.

The reason that this meditation is so powerful is that you work with sacred geometry, more specifically a shape that is known as the star-tetrahedron (see picture below). This is a symbol for divinity and its energy completely bypasses the logical mind. The star tetrahedron consists of two pyramids, one that points up and connects you to source, and one that points down and connects you to earth. Together they will balance you out completely and empower you.

I have been using the MerKaBa meditation since 1999 and have been teaching this now for many years. In my MerKaBa workshop we build a life-size star-tetrahedron. When people stand inside this shape they can usually feel the shift in energy inside them.

The star-tetrahedron

Part Three

Releasing your Emotions

20
It's all about emotions

Emotions play such an important role in your life and to your spiritual development, that I decided to dedicate a whole section of this book to it. In my experience as a healer, it is the one area that still does not get enough attention.

You are a walking storeroom full of emotions. You are holding within you a complete recollection of every event that ever happened in your life. Every emotion that you have ever felt, both positive ones (joy, contentment) and negative ones (pain, anger) are stored inside you. You are literally full of emotions.

Every illness is caused by your emotions

This may seem like a bold statement, but it is completely true. At least 95%, if not 99%, of all illnesses are caused by your stored emotions. How can this be? I can explain this in just three sentences:

1. If your immune system works perfectly it will keep your body completely healthy
2. The one thing that kills your immune system is stress
3. All stress is caused by your emotions

If you heal your emotions you will heal your body. This alone should be reason enough for anybody to want to completely release all the emotions they are carrying inside.

Have a look at the two pictures on the next page. The picture on the left is of a person who was wounded in life, who is full of emotions and most likely has a lot of physical problems.

The second picture is that of a normal, healthy person. The first big difference is that the major emotional blocks in the body have been released. The second is that there is a lot less mind activity. There is a direct relationship between the amount of emotions you are storing inside you and your mind activity. More on that later.

Your emotions are the key to your happiness

Which person is happier do you think: the person on the left or the person on the right? It is not hard to see that by healing your emotions you will become happier. That should be a second reason for you to make it a priority to heal all the negative emotions that you are holding inside you.

Your emotions prevent you from enlightenment

Now if you look at a person who is enlightened, the big difference is that they are completely empty. There are no thoughts. There are no stored emotions. You cannot have an empty mind if you are full of emotions. Emotions are like an anchor for your thoughts, it is impossible to let go of your thoughts if you don't let go of your emotions.

It is the emotions that you are holding inside you that are preventing you from enlightenment. This is perhaps the biggest missing element in the approach from teachers like Krishnamurti, Papaji, Mooji and Adyashanti. Just by raising your consciousness, which is in effect what they are trying to do, you will not reach enlightenment. You need to heal your emotions too.

21
How stress kills your body

To understand how stress literally kills your body, we need to go a little bit into the science of how your body works (in a palatable version).

The immune system

The first function of the body to look at is the immune system. This is the system that is designed to keep us healthy. It fights bacteria, viruses, fungi, it makes repairs to damaged cells and it destroys unwanted (cancer) cells. If your immune system works perfectly, you will not get ill.

The immune system needs a lot of energy to do it's job. This explains that when you are tired for a long period of time, you will get a cold, or get that flu that is going around, while your partner who is fit does not get the flu at all. It's just that your immune system does not have enough energy to do it's job and fight off the flu virus.

Stress

The second aspect to look at is stress. What exactly is stress? Physiological stress (the type of stress that causes illness and disease) happens when our nervous system is out of balance. To understand this we need to look at the Autonomic Nervous System (ANS). The ANS controls what is going on in your body. It's called autonomic because it happens automatically without the need to think about it. You don't have to think "I need to digest the food in my small intestine", or "bother, I need to repair these broken cells in my fingernails", it all gets done automatically by your body.

The ANS consists of two main parts: The first is the Parasympathetic Nervous System (PNS), which is in charge of growth, healing and maintenance, basically all the normal body functions. The PNS is in control most of the time. It also controls the immune system.

But when the "fire alarm" goes off, when there is a lot of stress, the Sympathetic Nervous System (SNS) takes over. This activates the "fight or flight" function of our body, just as your body would if you met a danger like a lion. When our body goes into fight or flight mode, it changes the blood flow (and energy flow) to those functions of the body that are needed to survive: mainly your muscles, as your body thinks that you will need to run away from the lion. Your body will stop digesting your food or repairing broken cells, because if you don't manage to run away from the lion there will be no need to do any of that any more. Cells don't get the nutrition and energy they need, waste products and toxins do not get removed. Everything stops except what is necessary to survive. It also stops you from sleeping for example, as you need to run away from the lion, not sleep!

The fight or flight mode is a brilliant function of the body, and it can save your life in the case of an emergency. But the problem is that the average person has so much stress, that their body stays in fight or flight mode for long periods of time. When that happens, the immune system gets weakened, cells do not get maintained and repaired anymore and they become weakened. Some cells die and the weakest link in your body will break. In other words: you get ill.

So we can summarise this as follows:
Stress in your system causes the "fire alarm" to go off. The SNS activates the "fight or flight" function of your body, and the immune system gets weakened. Your immune system does not get enough energy to keep all your cells in your body healthy. The weakest link in your body will break and you develop an illness.

Emotions

Stress is caused by your emotions. It is your emotions that activate the "fire alarm", the fight or flight function. You can understand how this work by looking at the two primal emotions that cause stress:

- Fear – this triggers the body response: I need to run away from that lion!
- Pain – this triggers the body response: I got hurt, I need to run away from this lion that is hurting me.

Both fear or pain can turn into anger. Note that anger is not a primary emotion, as there is a mind activity involved in it.

Anger triggers the body response: I am going to fight that lion!

It is totally valid to experience these emotions, but if you don't release these emotions and store them instead, you are storing this energy, and your body stays locked in this fight or flight state. Let's look more at how we store emotions in the next chapter.

22
Storing emotions

"What you suppress controls you"
Unknown

It may sound incredible, but everything that happens in your life is stored in your memory. Literally everything! Events from pre-birth when you are still in the womb, your birth, babyhood, childhood… a complete memory of every event in your life is stored inside of you.

You store every bit of information from all of your five main senses: what you were seeing, hearing, tasting, touching and smelling. You also store the emotions that you were experiencing!

The main senses that we use are visual and hearing, and when you think of a memory this is normally the first information that comes back. You remember what the beach looked like where you used to go on holiday. You remember the sound of the waves crashing on the beach, the happy shouts of children playing in the sea, it brings back the happy feelings from that time.

Memories can be triggered when you see or hear something. For example, when you hear a song on the radio from your childhood that you have not heard for years, it can take you straight back to that time in your life.

But the triggers can be other things as well. Smell for example, can be a very strong trigger. I remember one occasion when this happened. A few years after my first relationship, I was going to work on a tram, when at some point a woman boarded. When she walked past me I smelled her perfume – it was exactly the same perfume that my girlfriend used to wear. It triggered my memory and I was transported back in time. Lots of memories and emotions of my time with her came back to the surface.

It can happen with feelings (body sensations) too. The first time that I got a car with heated seating, something very funny happened. When I turned the heating on my bottom started getting nicely warm and it triggered a memory from when I was a baby: I was wearing a nappy with a warm poo inside it. I could even remember the smell...

Where do we store our memories?

Traditionally we are taught that our memory is located in our brain. But we are now learning that the memory function is far more complex than that.

There are an increasing number of cases reported where people inherit memories after having an organ transplant from a donor. This seems to suggest that memory is stored in our body, in our organs. Here is one example, taken from a news story:

"A transplant patient has developed an insatiable craving for junk food - after receiving a new heart from a teenager with a taste for fatty snacks.
David Waters is the latest example of an extraordinary phenomenon which sees some transplant recipients take on the characteristics of the donor. Before being given the heart of 18-year-old Kaden Delaney, who was left brain dead after a car crash, Mr Waters, 24, had no desire at all for Burger Rings, ring-shaped hamburger-flavoured crisps.
It was two years before he found out why the cravings had started suddenly after his operation. Kaden's family tracked him down to see who had benefited from their son's heart, and they began exchanging emails. A curious Mr Waters then asked: 'Did Kaden like Burger Rings? That's all I seemed to want to eat after my surgery.' He was astonished to hear that he ate them daily."
(Source: www.dailymail.co.uk)

This is just one example. So if our memory was only stored in the brain, why would we inherit memories (and character traits) when we receive a new heart or kidney? It's because our memory is stored in our body. And it is our whole body, not just in our heart like in this example. This phenomenon happens with every kind of transplant; whether it's a kidney, a liver, a blood transfusion... In fact recent research suggests that memory is stored in every cell of our body.

Each emotion has a certain location in the body

Clinical observation by doctors and healers shows that certain emotions are correlated to certain parts of our body. For example people whose lives are ruled by anger suffer from liver and gal bladder troubles.

The first person that I learned this from is Louise Hay. In her book *"You Can Heal Your Life"*, she published an extensive list of physical problems and the corresponding emotional issue.

Some examples of this correlation are given below:

    Anger = liver / gallbladder
    Fear = kidney / bladder
    Betrayal = heart / small intestine
    Grief = lungs / colon

Time heals all wounds?

You often hear that "time heals all wounds", but does it? This is one of these fallacies that sounds good, but are not actually true. In fact what is happening is that as time goes by, we bury our emotions deeper and deeper in our body and in our subconscious. Time does not heal our wounds, we just cover up the wound. Just like can happen when you get a splinter in your finger, if it went too deep it does not come out, but rather it gets covered by new skin, by scar tissue. It is the same for emotional wounds.

With the passing of time we "forget" the negative emotions, we forget the "bad stuff." This is why it is that when we think back to a certain period in the past of our lives, we get a real feeling of nostalgia. We only remember the good parts and it seems that it was such a great time. While in reality during this time there was just as much boredom, frustration, stress and suffering as there is in the current phase of your life.

This is actually a very clever coping mechanism. Can you imagine if you still remembered and felt the impact of all the emotional wounds that happened in the past? You would be in constant suffering. So instead we bury the emotions, we "forget" the bad stuff, and this allows us to move on with our lives and function normally.

This mechanism is called "repression" or "splitting" in psychological terms. It is like you are "splitting off" a certain part of yourself, and this often happens when a severe trauma happens. A typical example of this is when a young girl gets raped. This has such a deep emotional impact, that her system literally completely represses all memories and emotions of the event. It is the only way for her to cope. By the time she is an adult and comes to see me as a client, she has no idea at all that there was ever an abuse. Only certain symptoms might give away that something happened in childhood. It might take several years of therapy before the person is finally ready to allow the truth to come out. Without this "repression" mechanism she would literally not survive, she would not be able to cope with life, she would go mad.

Although this "repression" mechanism is a necessary and useful mechanism, it does have negative side effects. We have seen that stored emotions can develop into an illness. But there is another negative aspect of this mechanism:

It takes energy to keep your emotions suppressed.

It is as if you are trying to keep a balloon at the bottom of the swimming pool. It naturally wants to float to the surface, so you need to keep applying pressure to keep it down. This takes energy. It is exactly the same with emotions: they want to come to the surface, but our system keeps them locked down. This takes energy. The more emotions you are keeping down, the more emotions you are suppressing, the more energy you are using. It makes you tired and you need more sleep. It also means that your immune system has less energy available to keep you healthy. You are more prone to catch a cold or virus. You are more likely to get ill. You are aging quicker.

The opposite is true as well. If you release the emotions inside of you, you don't need to use all this energy to keep them "locked down." You get more energy, you need less sleep, your immune system has more energy, your body gets healthier, you will feel better and you don't age so much.

How pure is a baby?

In part two I said that when a baby is born it is pure. But exactly how pure is a baby? Maybe a baby is not as pure and empty as we may think.

First of all we have stored memories of our birth. The process of storing memories does not start when we are born, it starts from the moment the soul enters the embryo (roughly three months after conception).

My ex-wife Leona once had regression therapy, in which she went back to her birth. During the session she remembered clearly that when she was born she was not ready. She felt totally outraged that she was "pushed out." She didn't want to come out, she was not ready. All these emotions were stored, and she could still access them in her regression. Some time after this session she asked her mum about her birth. Her mum told her that she was overdue and that the hospital gave her an injection to induce the labour. It totally matched her experience of her birth.

Going a bit further back in time is the pregnancy itself. We are literally so linked to our mother that we often store the emotions that our mother is experiencing during the pregnancy.

So we have memories from birth, we have memories from the pregnancy. But there is more. We even have memories from past lives. So when we are born we are not a clean sheet. When we are born we already store a lot of memories and energies inside us, and these energies will have an effect on how our life will unfold.

23
Your emotions rule your mind

So far I have focussed on the impact that your stored emotions have on your physical body. But there is another aspect that is just as important to understand: your emotions rule your mind

How your mind works

In Part Two I have explained that our mind is just like an iceberg – our conscious mind is the tip of the iceberg, maybe 10% or even less. The majority of mind activity is happening under water in our subconscious mind.

Everything that happens in your life (*yes literally everything!*) is recorded in your subconscious. When you think of a memory, information about a past event is brought from your subconscious to your conscious mind.

Where do thoughts come from?

Now here is a question for you: Do you know what your next thought will be? And where does it come from? It seems like an impossible question to answer. In fact, the question "what will your next thought be?" creates a Catch 22 situation and causes your brain to freeze.

Brain research has discovered that our thoughts originate from our subconscious and "bubble up" to the surface and enter our conscious mind.

You may have observed this process in action for yourself. For example: sometimes you try to remember the name of a person, or the name of a song. You nearly get it, it is at the tip of your tongue, but the answer is just out of reach. Have you noticed that when you stop trying to remember, sometime later the answer just popped into your head? What happened there is that whilst you stopped trying to find the memory with your conscious mind, your subconscious mind continued searching your memory. When it found the answer it presented it to your conscious mind - the answer "popped up" into your head.

We can illustrate this process as follows:

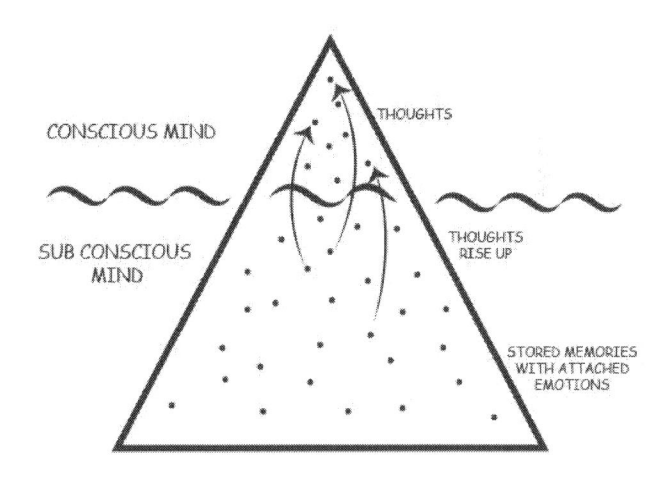

And we are always thinking of something! Our mind is constantly busy: observing what is happening, judging what is going on, going over the past, thinking of the future... It is never still. When you try to be still and meditate, thoughts keep coming in, bubbling up from your subconscious.

Emotions anchor your memories

A key to let go of your thoughts is to let go of your stored emotions. Emotions function like an anchor, keeping hold of the memories (thoughts).

You can observe this for yourself. The events that you can remember from your childhood are the situations that have a high emotional charge. These can be "good" or "bad" memories, the principle is the same. Mundane events that have no real emotional charge you will have forgotten, which only means that they do not surface to your conscious mind so easily.

To let go of your thoughts you need to let go of your emotions

When you let go of the emotional charge of past events they will not surface to your mind anymore. Your mind will become more still and you will become more empty, more at peace.

It is hard to be happy, to be truly at peace, whilst you are still storing all the pain, all the hurt, all the fears, all the wounds of your childhood and your life up to now inside you.

If you want to have peace of mind, you can meditate all you want, but the only way to truly achieve real mental peace is to release your stored emotions. As long as you keep this emotional charge inside you, it will always continue to bring up more thoughts.

But your stored emotions play an even bigger role in your life. Not only do they create every illness in your body, and create your thoughts, in fact your stored emotions create your whole life.

24
Your emotions create your life

Everything is energy

We have seen in Part Two that everything is energy. Your body is just energy spinning around really fast. Your thoughts are energy, and it is the same with emotions – your emotions are energy. Each emotion has a certain frequency and has a certain strength.

Emotions that we label as "negative" (fear, anger, pain) have a lower frequency than "positive" emotions such as joy and happiness.

When an emotion gets stuck at a certain place in the body, it is sitting there vibrating at a certain frequency. This frequency will affect the cells in the body where it is located, they start vibrating at the same frequency. This is called resonance. It is the same principle of a tuning fork.

You are a tuning fork

If you hold up two tuning forks and you strike the first one, it starts oscillating at a certain frequency, it starts sending out sound waves, energy waves. The second tuning fork will pick up these waves through the air and will start oscillating as well.

This same principle applies to us. You might have experienced the following scenario. You are at home and you are feeling ok, you are calm and in a good mood. But then your partner comes home and he or she is in a very irritable mood. Within minutes you will start to feel irritated as well. You have picked up the "irritation" energy waves, and your body is starting to resonate on that frequency.

Resonance does not have to be a bad thing, the opposite can happen as well. I remember working in a big office in Amsterdam. One rainy Monday morning I came into work and stepped into the elevator. It was quite full, and everybody was in the typical Monday morning mode: a bit glum and not very happy to be there. Nobody spoke a word. But then my colleague Alison stepped into the elevator. She had a big smile on her face and was beaming with a happy and bubbly energy. Within a minute the whole energy changed and by the time we got to the 11th floor, everyone was smiling and feeling better. Here energy literally shook out the Monday blues from all of us.

You create your own reality

You may have heard this before: *we create our own reality*. It sounds great, and we are happy to accept this when things go right in our life: "I have attracted this new job!" But it is much harder to accept when things don't work out. What if you cannot find a new job? What if you are unable to find a boyfriend? You start thinking: "I am trying so hard – why does it not work? I am visualising, I am sending it love, doing daily affirmations, but still nothing. What is going on? Maybe this "you create your own reality" stuff is not true."

But we are creating our own reality. We are creating all the time, 24/7. In fact it is not possible to not create. You are always emitting a certain energy, a certain frequency, and the universe is responding to that: like attracts like. You are getting back that what you are sending out. Or in other words:

Your energy is reflected in the world outside you. Everything that happens outside of you is a reflection of what is going on inside of you. Everything!

You will probably have observed this already. You can see that a person who has a lot of anger inside him, always seems to attract situations that will bring out that anger. Just as he finally sees a free parking space, someone else just takes it. When he finally does manage to park his car (after having to go in that expensive parking lot) he has to wait 20 minutes for a free table in the restaurant. Then the waiter takes ages taking his order…

And you will know the opposite kind of person. They seem to have luck on their side. Somehow they always manage to find a parking space. People are always kind to them. A table in the restaurant just becomes available. Life is flowing.

The real secret

Here is the catch: the energy that you are sending out is not just your positive thoughts, your affirmations. Remember the iceberg: 90% of your memories, your beliefs and your emotions are stored in your subconscious. But just because it is under water doesn't mean it is not sending out energy. It always is. What this means is that your conscious mind is only a small part of you as a creator. Your stored emotions are creating your reality.

Here is an example from my own life: As a young boy I was bullied at school. I had red hair, wore glasses, was the smartest kid in class, so there was plenty of ammunition. I got called names and the cool kids didn't want to play with me. I felt rejected. Somehow after a year or so the bullying stopped (after I decided that their behaviour was stupid and I didn't want to even be friends with them). But the energy of rejection was stored inside me. So when I was a teenager and started to get interested in girls guess what happened? I always got rejected.

The energy, the emotions that are stored in your subconscious determine your reality. This is why affirmations don't work all the time.

If a river has a very strong current and it is flowing south, you can try to swim upstream, to get to the north, but it will be a struggle, you won't get very far. Your subconscious is that river. If your subconscious holds a poverty frequency, you can try to create abundance with positive thinking all you want, but not much will happen. But when you clear the emotions, when you become empty, the river becomes a still pond. Now you can swim in any direction you choose.

Emotional patterns

Often trapped emotions can cause certain patterns in our life. Once a certain energy is stuck inside us it will be emitting that frequency, and this will attract situations in your life that will bring up the same frequency, the same emotion. What you are sending out is what you attract. I will illustrate this using an example from my own life.

After I separated from my wife I was doing a lot of healing. I realised that I had developed a pattern where I let myself be overpowered by women, just like happened between my ex-wife and myself. I wanted to find out what was at the core of this and started remembering times in my life when I experienced this feeling of being overpowered. Starting in the now and working back further and further in time, I came up with the following list (slightly abridged):

- Relationship with my ex-wife
- A previous relationship
- When I was 14 years old, a boy in the swimming pool sat on my neck "for fun" and pushed me under the water for a long time (I nearly drowned)
- When I was 4 my mum used to put my head under the tap to "cool me down" when I had a tantrum.

Then I checked how strong the stored emotion was on a scale from 0 to 10 (10 being the maximum). The near drowning incident scored a 9, not unsurprisingly. But I was shocked to discover that putting my head under the tap scored a 10. This was a total surprise to me, as this was a story that was mentioned sometimes at home and I always thought that it was a funny way to deal with the situation. But now I realised that for the little boy it was traumatic. I was truly overpowered - by a woman. This emotion was so strong, that once it got stored it created a pattern of events in my life. And all this was happening subconsciously.

By releasing the trapped emotions (I will explain how to do this later on) we change the energy inside us, and therefore we break the pattern.

Right after I released all these emotions, Leona (my ex-wife) noticed a change inside of me. When she came into the room she said "Wow what have you done? You are much more in your power." She had no idea that I had been working on myself. Later, when I was in a new relationship, the dynamic was a complete reversal of the usual pattern – this time I was the one "in charge", and my girlfriend was the "needy" one. It was a totally new experience for me. I had broken the pattern.

I have seen this time and time again presented in my work with clients. Often there is a situation during early childhood that has a major emotional impact. This does not have to be something horrific, but little children experience events very differently from adults (like my "head under the tap" situation). Once this traumatic energy is stored in the body, it starts a chain of events, it creates a certain pattern in the life of this person. When this has happened, you can do affirmations and positive thinking all you want, but only by removing the stored emotions will you free yourself from the past and be able to break the cycle. More examples of this will follow later in the book.

This is what emptiness is about. When you are empty, when you have released your past emotions, you are free. You will literally be free from your past.

So how can you release your stored emotions? I will look at this in the next Chapter.

25
Releasing emotions

The good news is that these days there are a lot of approaches available to release stored emotions. The bad news is that it can be completely overwhelming to decide what method to choose.

Some popular methods

Here is a list of some of the most popular methods, and also some lesser know ones:

- EFT (tapping)
- The Healing Code
- The Emotion Code
- Recapitulation
- Ho'oponopono

Below is a brief description of each method, along with some personal observations. There are many more methods that have sprung up in the past decade, but this list will already give you plenty to choose from.

EFT

EFT stands for Emotional Freedom Technique, and is also known as "tapping." This is probably the most widely used method. With EFT you resolve issues by tapping with your finger tips on 9 specific places (meridian points) on your body. It is a bit like acupuncture, but without the needles. The idea is that by tapping these points you rebalance the energy flow in the body. The complete instructions for using EFT are available for free at: www.emofree.com.

The Healing Code

With The Healing Code you release emotions by visualising that you shine light out of your fingers to four specific places on your face, and stating a positive affirmation to counteract the negative emotion that is stored.

The Emotion Code

With The Emotion Codes you release emotions by moving a magnet over your head and spine (central meridian) whilst setting the intention to the release the emotion.

From my own experience The Emotion Code is a much more effective technique than EFT or The Healing Code. The Healing Code works, but it can be time consuming. Sometimes I needed to do sessions twice a day for a week before an emotion was completely resolved.

In my personal experience, EFT seems to work more on the surface level. Rebalancing the energy in your body will improve your symptoms, but it may not always release the core issue. This might then resurface again and further sessions are needed.

With The Emotion Code I am able to remove an issue using magnets within a single session in a few minutes. It really does remove the core emotional issue from your body. By working with a magnet you can "manipulate" your memory much more effectively, this is because memories seem to be stored using the magnetic field of the body. I will explain this in more detail in a later chapter.

Recapitulation.

This is a lesser known, but effective technique from the Mexican Toltec Shamanic tradition. It works by focussing on past events in your life, breathing in the energy (power) that you gave away when this event happened. You then breathe out any energies that you have taken on from other people. I will describe this technique more in a later chapter.

Ho'oponopono

This comes from the Hawaiian shamanic tradition and works by repeating a short prayer/affirmation to release emotions that are stored in you. Ho'oponopono became famous in the west after one practitioner cured a whole hospital ward of mentally ill criminals - just by working on himself. The philosophy behind it is beautiful, which I will explain it in a later chapter.

Finding the underlying emotion

I have talked a lot about releasing the emotion that causes a certain problem, but how do you know what this emotion is? When you have persistent headaches for example, how do you find out where this comes from? The answer is: your body can tell you. This is because everything that has ever happened to you is stored in your body memory. Imagine that you could ask your body what caused your headaches. Imagine that your body could answer you and tell you exactly why you are having these headaches. This is exactly what you can do using Kinesiology.

Kinesiology, or Applied Kinesiology to be more precise, is also known as "muscle testing." It works as follows:

Your body knows what is true or not. Kinesiology is based on the discovery that when you make a statement that is true, your body (muscles) will be stronger. When you make a statement that is false, your body (muscles) will be weaker.

A commonly know test is the "arm-pull-down test", where the patient extends one arm and the practitioner presses down on the arm. When the practitioner asks a question that is true, the arm stays strong (and horizontal), when the answer is false the arm goes weak and moves down. By asking questions with "yes" or "no" answers, the practitioner can find out what the cause of an issue is.

A similar method that I prefer is the "sway test." It is based on the principle that we tend to move toward the truth and tend to move away from falsehoods. The patient will stand in a neutral position. When I ask a question that is true, the patient's body will start to sway forward a little. When I make a statement that is false the body moves backwards. What I like about this method is that there is no physical involvement by the practitioner, and it is less tiring for the patient. Keeping your arm outstretched for some time can lead to tiredness and incorrect test results. In my experience, the sway test gives more accurate feedback.

Here is an example to illustrate how I use body testing.
Let's use a 36 year old woman with persistent headaches as an example. My line of questioning could go as follows:

Q: Are the headaches caused by an emotional issue?
A: Yes
Q: When did this occur. Younger than 16 years?
A: Yes
Q: Younger than 8 years?
A: Yes
Q: Younger than 4 years?
A: No
Q: 5 years old?
A: Yes
So we now know that something happened when she was 5 years old.
Q: Was it to do with the family?
A: Yes
Q: Was it to do with the mother?
A: Yes

Basically, you keep asking questions to find out what you need to know about the situation. Then you determine what the emotions are that were stored. For this purpose I use a list of the most common emotions. For example:
Q: Is the stored emotion Fear?
A: No
Q: Is the stored emotion Anger?
A: Yes

We don't always need to know exactly what happened. In fact often the body (subconscious) will keep certain events blocked. Often knowing what emotion causes the headaches is enough to be able to release it.

Note that the above example is only used to illustrate the principle of how you can find out information using body testing. Please ensure you receive proper training before starting to use this method, especially when you want to work with other people. I cannot emphasise this enough. You could unknowingly open up a suppressed trauma and trigger all kinds of reactions in the patient, even a complete breakdown. Imagine that you start with an "innocent" headache, and next thing you find out that the woman you are working with was raped by her father when she was 7 years old. I have had situations like this in my practise. Would you be able to handle that?

Kinesiology can be a very useful tool, and used properly you can find out a lot of information. For example:
- You can ask your body if a certain food that you are eating is good for it.
- You can use it to find out what is causing an allergic reaction.

The possibilities are endless, but there are also limitations: you can only ask the body about things that have happened in the past, or that are happening now. Your body does not know the future. Therefore asking whether you should buy this house or that one, will not give valid results. Sadly enough you also can't use it to predict the winning lottery numbers.

In the next chapters I will describe in more detail a few techniques for releasing emotions: Recapitulation, Ho'oponopono and The Emotion Code. My aim is not to give a complete "training manual" on how to use these methods, but to give enough information for you to make up your mind whether this is something you would like to learn or experience. These are the methods that I use personally (and I have tried a lot of other methods out there). They work. But just because it resonates with me doesn't mean that it resonates for everyone. Find the method that works for you.

26
Recapitulation

Recapitulation is a technique from the Mexican Toltec Shamanic tradition, and has been described by Carlos Castaneda, Taisha Abelar and Victor Sanchez.

The purpose of recapitulation is to take back your personal power that you have given away to people, places and things, often during unpleasant or traumatic events in your life. Taking back your energy and your power strengthens your energy body, and releases you from the old events that have caused you emotional pain. As your power is returned to you, you will find your life becoming more joyous and free.

Recapitulation is based on the understanding that we have luminous energy "filaments", or energy cords, extending from ourselves to others. These connections form when we direct our attention and energy outward. They also form when others place their attention and energy on us.

In recapitulation we look at our energy connections and decide which ones to keep or cultivate, and which ones are not in our best interest. We can then manage our energy connections, stop parasitic energy drains and recover stagnant energy.

The Sweeping Breath

The basic steps for recapitulation are as follows:

1. Find a private space where you can work without interruption. Make sure that you won't be disturbed by family members, phones, or other distractions.

2. Remove your shoes. This is important so that the energetic connection between your body and the earth will be stronger.

3. Sit in a comfortable upright position, either in a straight-backed chair or, if you have more flexibility, using the Lotus position on the floor. If your body is flexible enough, you might want to try the traditional "Toltec Dreamer" position, where you sit on the floor and hug your knees to your chest, allowing your head to rest on your knees.

4. Choose an incident to work on. In your mind, bring back that incident to memory with as much detail as possible. See the decorations in the room or the scenery outdoors, hear any sounds, smell any smells - allow all of your senses to participate, until it feels like you are back in that experience.

5. Allow any emotions to arise naturally, without restraint or judgment. As much as possible, become an observer, a detached witness, observing the emotions and events without letting them overwhelm you.

6. When you feel fully present in this event, begin pulling your power back by using the Sweeping Breath:

- Feel, and if possible see, the energy strands or "fibres" that connect your solar plexus to the memory.

- Turn your head to the right, keeping your mind fully focused on the memory.

- Turning your head slowly from right to left, inhale deeply through your nostrils. This breath is pulling back your energy that was lost during the incident. At the same time, feel your energy fibres pulling your personal power back into your solar plexus.

- Next turn your head slowly from left to right, blowing out through your mouth any energy that isn't yours (i.e. emotions or words from other people, anything that isn't your personal power).

- Continue doing the sweeping breath until the memory feels "neutral", until you feel no more emotion of any kind.

- At this point, you will want to sever your connection with that memory. Without breathing, turn your head quickly from right to left and back again. This acts as a "scissor" to cut the energetic cords that attach you to the memory.

- At the same time, feel the cut energy fibres from your solar plexus being completely pulled back into your body. The other cut end, attached to the memory, withers and is grounded into the Earth.

Making an Inventory

In the Toltec tradition students are asked to make a complete list of all the events and situations in their life to recapitulate. This is called the Inventory.

A good idea is to begin your list by creating sections for "Lovers", "Family Members", "Friends & Acquaintances", "Work", "Personal Beliefs", etc. Other sections may come to you as you do the work.

Many Toltec teachers recommend beginning with your lovers, since that tends to be the area in our life where we lose the most energy. Start by listing all of the lovers who pop into your mind, with a brief note about your feelings and beliefs about each one, along with memories of that person that cause you grief, shame, anger or other unpleasant emotions. These so-called "negative" emotions indicate that you lost power during one or more interactions with the person.

When your list of lovers is complete, you move on to the next part, perhaps for Family & Friends, etc. It is not necessary to do one section at a time, but it does make this process easier for some people.

In the Toltec tradition making the Inventory is the first step, but you can begin recapitulating your daily life right away, using the Sweeping Breath technique given above.

The old Toltec masters required their apprentices to recapitulate their entire lives, a process that can take months if not years. This was done sitting in a special cave, or in a special wooden box. My guess is that you are probably not in a position to lock yourself away in a cave for a year, nor will you have any desire to do so. But you can start working on the most important issues from your life, or whatever issue comes up for you at present.

Some people make this a daily practise. You can recapitulate everyday annoyances at the end of the day, before you go to sleep. This allows you to take back any power lost in daily events, and frees you from connections with interpersonal drama.

Personally I use this technique either when I have no magnets to hand (so I can't use The Emotion Code), or in situations where I clearly feel that I have given my energy and power away to another person. It works beautifully.

For more information I suggest you to read: "*The Toltec path of recapitulation: healing your past to free your soul*" by Victor Sanchez.

27
Ho'oponopono

"Ho-wottie?" you may ask. It is pronounced "Hoo-O-Ponno-Ponno", and is an ancient sacred healing method from Hawaii. It was traditionally performed by a Kahuna (Hawaiian shaman). Ho'oponopono gained fame in the west after one initiate, Dr Ihaleakala Hew Len, cured a whole ward of mentally ill criminals in a state prison hospital in Hawaii. That in itself is an incredible feat, but the most remarkable thing was that he did this without ever working directly with the patients, he only worked on himself! Here is that story.

The Ho'oponopono story

In the eighties there was a special ward at the Hawaii State Hospital, a high-security psychiatric clinic for mentally ill criminals. People who had committed extremely serious crimes (murder, rape, kidnapping) were sent there when they had a very deep mental disorder.

It was a terrible place to be in. All seclusion rooms were occupied by violent patients. Many patients had to be shackled by the ankles and wrists. Violence in the unit, by patients against patients, or by patients against staff was a daily occurrence. Doctors and nurses were so frightened that they would walk close to the walls if they saw an inmate coming their way in the corridor. The inmates would never be brought outside to get fresh air because of their relentless aggressive attitudes. The scarcity of staff was a chronic issue: sick leave and staff turnover was very high due to the stress and terrible working environment. It was in intense, volatile and depressing place. The atmosphere was so bad that even plants didn't grow, and the paint kept peeling off the walls.

One day, a newly appointed clinical psychologist, Dr. Hew Len, arrived at the ward. Often psychologists would come and go, after getting frustrated that their work did not have any effect on the inmates. But this man was different from the other psychologists who had worked there before. In fact, he didn't seem to be doing anything at all, except just turning up and always being cheerful and smiling in a very natural, relaxed way. From time to time he would ask for the files of the inmates. He never saw them personally though. He just sat in his office, looked at their files, and to members of the staff who showed an interest he would tell them about a weird thing called Ho'oponopono.

Little by little things started to change in the hospital. Medication levels started to be reduced. Some prisoners could start walking without being shackled. One day somebody tried again to paint those walls, and this time it actually stayed on, making the environment more palatable. The gardens started being taken care of. Some tennis courts were repaired and some prisoners, that up until then would never be allowed to go outside, started playing tennis with the staff, including Dr. Hew Len. More and more prisoners obtained permission to go outside unshackled, without causing trouble to the hospital's employees.

In the end, the atmosphere changed so much that the staff were not on sick leave any more. Actually, more people than needed now worked there. Prisoners started to be released. Dr. Hew Len worked there for three years. In the end, there remained only a couple of inmates that were relocated somewhere else, and the clinic for the mentally insane criminals was closed down.

So how is this possible? How can just one man cure a whole ward of mentally ill criminals, just by working on himself? To understand this you must learn the three core principles of Ho'oponopono.

The three core principles of Ho'oponopono

The first principle is: *Change what's inside of you and you will change the world outside of you.*

The second principle is: *You are 100% responsible for everything that happens in your life.*

The third principle is: *You clean your energy (your stored emotions) by saying:*

> *"I am sorry*
> *Please forgive me*
> *Thank you*
> *I love you"*

It may sound very simple, and it is, but it is also hugely profound. Let's look at these principles in more detail.

Change what's inside you and you will change the world outside you

We all know the saying "Be the change you want to see", but this literally is true. Ho'oponopono recognises that the energy inside us is attracting the events in our life, the world outside us is a reflection of the energy inside of us. I have discussed this principle earlier in this chapter.

The second principle follows on from the first:

You are 100% responsible for everything that happens in your life

It is a logical consequence of the first principle; if the world outside you is a reflection of the energy inside you, then it means that you are 100% responsible for everything that happens in your life.

This is both a very exciting idea, but also terrifying. You are responsible for everything. *Everything!*

Your boss is a tyrant? It's your responsibility.
Your children are not good students? It's your responsibility.
There is a war going on and you feel bad because you are a good person, a pacifist? The war is your responsibility.
You see that children around the world are hungry and malnourished, if not starving? Their want is your responsibility.

There are no exceptions. The world is literally your world, it is your creation. If something shows up in your world, it means that on some level it resonates with the energy inside of you.

It is this principle that Dr Hew Len was using when he cured the ward of mentally ill criminals. In Dr Hew Len's own words: "I was simply healing the part of me that created them." He was reading the files of the criminals. As he was reading what they had done, he noticed what emotions were being triggered inside of him. Anger for example. He knew that the anger is the emotion that he was sharing with the criminal patient. Then he started the healing on himself, taking full responsibility for what was going on with a given patient. He started clearing his anger. As his anger got cleansed, the anger in the patient was reduced. He continued this process until all anger was released. Violence reduced in the hospital, shackles could be removed, and finally the patients were totally cured. That's how those people got better, because their doctor had the strange view that it was himself who needed the healing, not them.

The Ho'oponopono prayer

> *"I am sorry*
> *Please forgive me*
> *Thank you*
> *I love you"*

The word "Ho'oponopono" means: to rectify an error. How do you heal yourself with Ho'oponopono? There are four steps involved in using this prayer.

First you recognise that whatever comes to you is your creation, the outcome of bad memories (emotions) buried inside you.
Secondly you regret whatever errors of body, speech and mind caused those bad memories: "I'm sorry."
Thirdly, by requesting the Divine Intelligence within yourself to release those memories, to set you free "Please forgive me, I love you."
Then lastly, of course, you say "Thank you."

You could read the prayer as follows: I'm sorry, please forgive me for whatever is going on inside of me that has created this (problem). Thank you, I love you.

Dr Hew Len explained what happens on an energetic level as follows: By saying the prayer you initiate the healing process with your conscious mind. Your subconscious mind will select what memories (emotions) are to be healed. This is presented to the divine, which will send healing love. It is this love that transmutes the emotion and replaces it with the frequency of love.

Here is another very different way to look at the Ho'oponopono effect. In Part Two, I discussed the effect of thoughts on water. Dr Masaru Emoto demonstrated this with his microscopic pictures of frozen water molecules (see the image below). If the impact of saying "I love you" is this big on water - can you imagine how large the impact will be on you if you replace your continuous mind activity (which is mostly thoughts based on fear) with "I love you?"

Case study: Rosa

Rosa came to me to help her release stored emotions. In the first session we were talking about her life, she told me that she lived in a nice house, and how she stored lots of items for her mother at her place. We had a good session and she left feeling much lighter, with her heart more open. When she came back the next week she told me that she had a chat with her mother a few days after our session. Her mother told her that she felt that she was now ready to let go of a lot of stuff she had in storage for many years. How beautiful this was! As Rosa was letting go of her (emotional) stuff, her mother was now ready to let go of her (physical) stuff too! This is exactly the effect I am describing in this chapter – when you change your inside, the world outside you changes as well. The cleaning that you do will ripple through and affect the people around you.

Applying Ho'oponopono in your life

There are lots of ways in which you can use Ho'oponopono, here is a list of ideas to get you going:

- Use it anytime there is a problem in your life. Remember that you are not trying to fix the external event (the other person), you are working to heal the memories (emotions) inside of you. You are always working on yourself.

- Repeat the prayer like a mantra every time you think of it. After a while your subconscious will take over and start playing this over and over again. Now you are on autopilot.

- There is a Ho'oponopono song on YouTube. It's a bit cheesy but it sticks in your brain!

- I love doing Ho'oponopono when I am cleaning the house, or weeding the garden. As I am cleaning my outside world, at the same time I am cleaning my inside.

- You can write the prayer down and put it under your pillow. Your subconscious knows that it is there and will take it in.

- Repeat the prayer the last ten minutes just before go to sleep. Your subconscious will receive the instruction that you want to repeat it, and keep running it in your (subconscious) mind during the night. I found that after a few days of doing this, whenever I woke up, the mantra was still in my head. Can you imagine what happens to your energy if your subconscious mind is repeating "please forgive me, I love you" all night long?

There is a lot more to say about Ho'oponopono than I can put in a few pages. There are several good books about Ho'oponopono, but my favourite one is *"Zero Limits"* by Joe Vitale.

28
The Emotion Code

The emotion code was developed by Dr Nelson Bradley. It works by using magnets to clear trapped emotions, by moving a strong magnet over your central meridian, along your spine, whilst holding the intention to release a specific emotion. I have found it to be much more effective than other methods like EFT or the Healing code. The key to understanding the power of the Emotion Code is to understand the role of magnets.

Memories and the magnetic field of the body

Magnetism and the link to our memory is a field that has not been well researched yet. What we do know is that magnetic energy is an intrinsic part of the body's natural processes. The following story is little known but nevertheless true. When the first astronauts who ever went into space came back to earth they suffered from memory loss. Nobody knew what had caused this. Only by a process of trial and error did NASA find out that it had to do with leaving the Earth's magnetic field. Once NASA replicated the earth's magnetic field in the space craft the problem did not reoccur. So somehow our memory is link to the earth's magnetic field.

We know that pigeons use the earth magnetic field to find their way home. There are known cases when there was a magnetic storm (a phenomenon where the earth magnetic field temporarily changes direction) which had the result that the pigeons flew to a different place. They lost their way as the magnetic field now pointed somewhere different.

You may know that when you hold a strong magnet next to your computer it will erase your computer's memory. The same applies for your credit card. (*Don't try this at home!*)

Scientist have discovered that all of the tissues and organs in the body produce a specific electro-magnetic field. But the heart is by far the most powerful organ of our body. The electromagnetic field of your heart extends to 8-12 feet from your body:

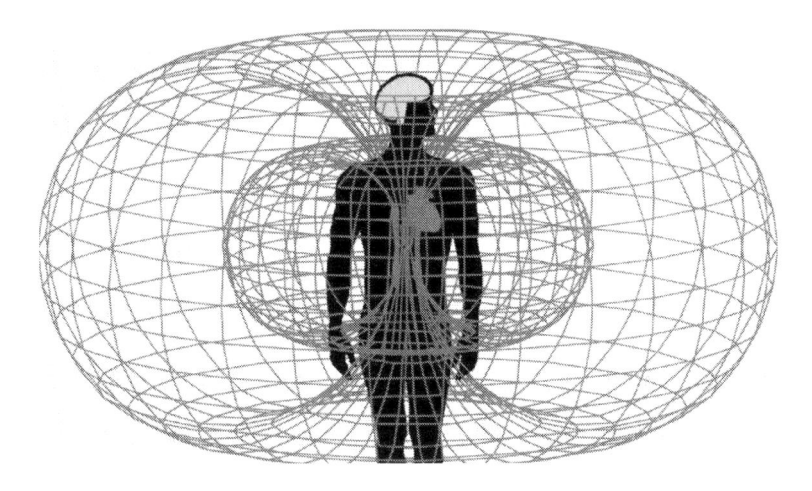

(picture copyright HeartMath Institute)

Scientists have measured that the heart is up to 100,000 times stronger electronically than the brain, and up to 5,000 times stronger magnetically than the brain. This is why the heart is so important. The issues of your heart are the most important issues to heal.

So there is an obvious link between magnetism and our memory. It seems that somehow we store memories using the body's magnetic field. So by accessing the magnetic field of your body, you access the memory. Maybe the simplest way to describe this is that magnets literally magnify your intentions. By combining the power of your intention with the power of magnets, we are able to cleanse memories very effectively.

What magnet to use

In principle, The Emotion Code works with any magnet, but obviously the stronger the magnet is, the stronger the field you will generate, and the easier it will be. When I first started testing The Emotion Code, I was trying to find the strongest magnet that I had in my house. In my case it was a magnet that I used to clean the glass of my fish tank. Initially I was a bit sceptical whether it would work with such an ordinary magnet, but much to my surprise it did!

Now I use a much more powerful and special magnet from Nikken, a Japanese company that specialises in magnet technology. Nikken have a whole range of magnetic products to enhance your well-being. The magnet that I use is the "Magboy." It is easy to hold in your hand and rolls comfortably over the body.

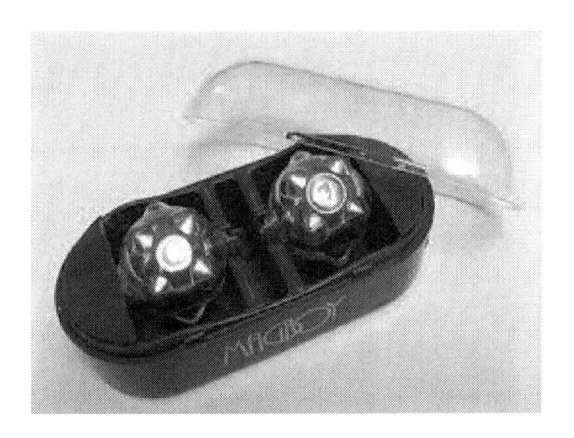

How it works

The basic procedure of The Emotion Code is as follows:

First you need to find out what the emotion is that causes the issue you are working on. Sometimes this is obvious, at other times you need to ask the body using kinesiology (as described on page 140).

Once you have determined what the emotion is, check how strong it is on a scale of 0 to 10 (10 being the strongest possible). Note that this is not a part of the Emotion Code instructions, but I find it useful to know.

You clear the emotion as follows:

First you set the intention to release the trapped emotion of ..... (for example Anger)

When you are healing yourself: move the magnet from in between your eye brows up and over your head, down to the base of your neck. Do this a few times. Depending on the strength of the magnet and the strength of the emotion you might need to run the magnet between three to ten times.

When you are healing others: move the magnet from the base of the neck down to the base of the spine. This is the great meridian. All meridians are connected to the great meridian, and the energy will flow to wherever it needs to go in the body. This is one of the things that I like about the Emotion Code, you don't need to find out where to work on the body or where to tap, it is a very simple procedure.

Once you have run the magnet a number of times, check whether you have completely released the emotion, by asking the body. Repeat the procedure if needed until you have completely released the trapped emotion.

Something that I find useful is to run the magnet from the top of the legs down to the ankles. This helps to move the energy that was released out of the body. (Note that this is not a part of the official Emotion Code Instructions).

Check if there are any other stored emotions related to the issue that you want to resolve. If there are, use the same process for these emotions as well.

In my experience, I am able to release an emotion within a few minutes. Once removed it really has gone, it does not resurface the next day or week (unlike a lot of other methods that I have tried).

What I have described here is the basic procedure for The Emotion Code. In the book "*The Emotion Code*" by Dr. Nelson Bradley, you will find more detailed information, special situations, lots of examples, flowcharts that guide you how to find an emotion, a chart of the most common emotions, how to work on animals and children, working via distance and much more. I highly recommend this book if you are interested in using the Emotion Code.

Some examples from my work with clients over the past few years are below. (*All names have been changed to protect the client's privacy.*)

Kevin

Kevin came to me to help him let go of a trauma from childhood. He grew up in a family with a lot of issues and had a very difficult childhood. One of the issues was that his father was verbally and emotionally aggressive towards him. As a result he could not deal with any form of anger or emotional aggression. He recently had an experience where he went for dinner at his girlfriend's family house. At some point during a discussion, her dad raised his voice and strongly disagreed with something that Kevin said. This triggered something in him and he started shaking. He was so affected that he had to leave.

Not surprisingly, there were a lot of strong emotions stored inside him from his childhood. As I was working with him he was literally changing in front of my eyes with every emotion that we took out. He felt much lighter after the 1st session. He had three sessions over the next two weeks. A couple of weeks after that he contacted me and told me that something incredible had happened. A man came into the shop where he worked and was very aggressive. His colleague in the shop actually hid away behind the counter. But Kevin was not affected at all, he remained calm and managed to sooth the man. He was amazed, "if this happened a month ago I would have fallen to pieces" he said. It was clear evidence that the emotional triggers had really been released.

Healing the cat

I was staying with a friend one time who has two beautiful cats. One of them however was very edgy. She was shy, and could be a bit aggressive, often biting her owner. I did not feel comfortable stroking her, which is very unusual for me as I really love cats.

My friend told me that she found her as a kitten in the forest and that she had always been needy and wanted to remain close to her. I offered to check what was going on with the cat, to see if she had emotions or a trauma trapped inside her. My friend held the cat and made a connection this way, whilst I asked questions in this manner, testing on my friend for the response. The moment we started the cat somehow knew what was going to happen and became very nervous. The cat did have trapped emotions, and we soon found out that she was abandoned by her previous owners in the forest as a kitten. She felt rejected and this scored a 10 out of 10 in terms of emotional impact. Every time I asked a question that was a "Yes" she would give a loud "Miaow!" She was actually telling us the answer!

As I removed the emotions with my magnet, I could feel waves of energy running down my spine. I told the cat she was loved and she noticeably relaxed. Then she jumped down and hid away. After a while she came out and slowly came to us. Soon my friend was playing with the cat, teasing her a bit, but she would not bite like before. I could feel that the edginess inside of her was now gone. The next day she came up to me, started rubbing her head against me and even jumped on my lap! She turned into a much calmer, more affectionate and happier cat.

Gary

Gary is six years old and is playing outside. When he crosses the street, all of a sudden a car comes at him at enormous speed. He knows it is going to hit him and he is terrified..... The next moment he wakes up. He is in a hospital bed, with all kind of tubes in him. He cannot talk and he cannot move. Breathing is difficult. He finds out that he is 8 years old and has just woken up from a coma that lasted one and a half years....

Gary is now 39 years old, He had to rebuild his life after the accident. He spent three years revalidating - learning to speak and to walk again, he had half of his lung removed, which affects his breathing and speech. He missed out on most of his childhood. He finished education and built a career in IT and the music industry. He is an incredibly brave and determined guy, but the accident still affects him every day. He shakes a lot and there is still a lot of tension in his system.

I offered to help him clear the emotions that are stored in his body from the accident. It turned out to be the most amazing healing session that I have ever witnessed.

I tuned into him and asked his body what emotions were stored from the accident. The first one was terror, and not surprisingly that scored 10 out of 10 in terms of emotional impact. As I was clearing the emotions using magnets, I got the image of the car coming at him and I could feel his terror at the time. In a few minutes his body had released this emotion of terror, and we moved on to the next emotion, which was shock.

As I took this emotion out I was talking to him, and information came through about why the accident happened; how he had chosen to have this experience in this life in order to remember how precious this life is, and how precious it is to have a body. Then all of a sudden he started trembling and shaking, first slowly, then it increased until it became so strong that I had to hold him quite tightly in an embrace to prevent him from falling over. I was checking to see if I needed to do anything but I felt that I just needed to let it happen. As I was holding him in a tight embrace I could feel the emotion running through me as well. Then all of a sudden he let out a big sigh and I felt a wave of energy go into the earth. The shaking stopped and his breathing returned to normal. I knew that all emotions from the accident had been released. All of a sudden there was a silence...

Gary was speechless, he felt a space in his head, a freedom and a peace that he had not felt before in his life. It was beautiful.

29
Some personal experiences

Below are some extracts from my diary, in which I describe some of my own experiences clearing my own emotions using The Emotion Code. It will give you an idea of what to expect during and after the healing sessions.

Working on myself (Session 1)

I decided to make a list of all the main events in my life that I can remember that had an emotional impact. That only took about half an hour. My plan is to release all these emotions in the next few weeks. I want to be free!

Tonight I cleaned the first events:

- My mum putting my head under the tap when I threw a tantrum (bless her!)
- Seeing a scene on the TV news when I was young, of fights and a man being attacked with a glass bottle
- Two memories of fighting with other kids when I was young
- One time when I was physically attacked when I went out at night (I was about 21)
- Memories of neighbours arguing (this happened a lot, their living room was next to my bedroom and I could hear their arguments word by word - this had a big impact on me)

Before I started I scored the impact of each memory on a scale 0 to 10, with 10 being the highest impact. I kept clearing the emotion with magnets until the score was down to zero. All these emotions were cleared in just half an hour. What I found is that once the emotion is released it's gone and doesn't come back. After the session I drank plenty of water, and it's amazing but I could actually feel lighter already!

Working on myself (Session 2)

Last night I did another round of clearing emotions:

- Three separate near drowning incidents (fear & confusion)
- The death of my mum. I was expecting the emotion to be grief, but surprisingly it was abandonment.
- Bullying. This scored 10 out of 10. When I was little I had red hair, I wore glasses and I was the smartest kid in class, so there was plenty of ammunition to attack me!

Again, it took just under 30 minutes to release all these emotions. Here is another part of last night's session:

The bullying scored an emotional impact of 10. This bullying happened at primary school and then again at secondary school. When I was 14 years old the bullying stopped. Although I coped quite well with it, and never felt that it had really damaged me much, what came up last night was the emotion of feeling rejected.

Then I had a major insight. As a teenager I never had a girlfriend, I was always rejected. I only had my first kiss when I was 19. The pattern repeated itself. I never realised the link with the bullying until last night! So in my clearing session this morning I worked through a list of eight different times where I was in love with a girl and was rejected. It shows how one incident starts a pattern in our lives that gets played out over and over again until we manage to break the cycle.

Working on myself (Session 3)

So how does it feel when I clear these emotions? Well this week I did three sessions. The first one lasted one hour, the second and third were half an hour long. By now I have cleared all the emotions from the main events up until my 21st birthday, or roughly halfway of my life. And I'm feeling fantastic!

During the sessions I experience mainly two sensations: the first is a feeling of light-headedness, sometimes followed by a mild headache. This goes away after a few hours. The second is that sometimes I get a knot in my shoulders. This slowly dissolves in a day or so. Directly after the session I literally feel lighter – it's hard to describe, but I feel more free somehow. After the 3rd session a feeling of euphoria came over me.

I noticed something else too. Right after the 1st session when I woke up the next morning I had a lot more energy than normal. This makes sense, as we use a lot of energy to keep these emotions suppressed. By releasing these emotions from our body we free up that energy.

Different people have different experiences, but the release process tends to be relatively light. This is not about hours of talking and reliving the emotions. Often you can see the changes in someone's face after the session: all tension is literally gone, and they can look ten years younger.

30
Conclusion

I have discussed three techniques that you can use to release stored emotions.

I use Ho'oponopono for general cleaning, just like hoovering your house. It works, Dr Hew Len's story is a powerful proof of that. The disadvantage of Ho'oponopono is that you have little control over the process. It's up to God (your soul) to decide exactly which memories will get cleared. In contrast, The Emotion Code is like a laser that allows you to target exactly the specific emotion and event that you want to remove. Recapitulation is great for situations where you feel that you have given your power away. But like I said at the beginning, there are lots of other techniques out there. Just find what resonates with you and do it!

Your stored emotions cause stress in your body. It's the stress in your body that creates illness. If you can release all the emotions that you are storing inside you, your body will heal itself, you will be super healthy.

Your stored emotions keep you locked in the past. They will keep re-creating similar experiences in your life. Your emotions will keep your mind locked in the past. Memories of past events will keep occupying your mind. By releasing your emotions you are literally freeing your self from the past.

The more empty you become, the lighter you will feel. It literally works like this: when you release the emotions of pain, fear, anger etc, you are removing lower frequencies from your system. As a result your frequency will go up. By emptying yourself you will literally start vibrating on a higher frequency – this is Bliss.

The more empty you become, the more space you create inside of you. When there is space your soul energy can come in more and more, and your frequency will go up even more. You are moving towards Bliss.

So release your emotions. You will feel lighter. You will feel free from the past. You will feel space. You will feel connected to your soul. You will feel bliss. Emptiness and Bliss, they go hand in hand.

Part 4

Raising your consciousness

31
Introduction

This last part of this book is about raising your consciousness. It is such an important aspect of spiritual development, that a lot of spiritual teachers, for example Krishnamurti, Adyashanti and Mooji, focus their teaching completely on this.

This part of the book consists of short chapters, each explaining a certain aspect. The topics in these chapters are what I find myself discussing time and time again with my clients. There are topics like: Luxury Problems, Acceptance, Forgiveness, The Illusion of Happiness, Letting go, Love, Fear, Why am I here...

These chapters are meant to be re-read, to be pondered upon, meditated upon. You can read a chapter on it's own, when you just want to look at a certain topic. But there is a flow to how this material is presented, taking you from your ego to your soul. It is meant to literally lift you into a higher state of consciousness as you go along. Let's start with an overview of the seven levels of consciousness...

32
Seven levels of consciousness

There are seven main levels of consciousness that people operate from. Once you understand what these are, you will start to recognise this in the people around you and in people in the media. These seven levels are:

1. Security:
   At this level the person is mainly preoccupied with food, shelter, or anything that creates a feeling of safety. This person will continuously try to get enough, in order to feel secure.

2. Sensations:
   The person on this level is trying to get happiness in life by having more and stronger pleasurable sensations and activities. For many people the ultimate pleasure is sex. But other addictions can be: food, drink, music, etc. for example.

3. Power:
   When you are operating on this level of consciousness you are concerned with dominating people, increasing your prestige, wealth, position and pride. This is often done via various means of hierarchy, manipulation and control (sometimes very subtle).

4. Love:
   At this level you are learning to live in the world with the feelings of harmony, to flow with life with acceptance of what is. You start to see yourself in everyone and everyone in yourself. You feel compassion for the people who are caught up in the drama of security, sensation and power. You are beginning to love everybody unconditionally, including yourself.

5. Friendly Reality:
   At this level you experience the friendliness of the world you are creating. You begin to realise that you have always lived in a perfect world. You will consciously work to let go of your addictions, to free yourself of your emotion-backed demands. The more you let go of these, the more you experience a continuous enjoyment of the here and now in your life, becoming more loving and accepting.

6. Conscious Self Awareness - The Watcher:
   At this level your conscious awareness is watching your body and mind perform on the five lower levels. You will experience non-judgment, as you witness the drama of your body and mind. You will observe your social roles and life games, free from fear.

7. Cosmic Awareness, Pure Awareness:
   At this ultimate level you have transcended self-awareness to become pure awareness. You are one with everything. You are love, peace, beauty, wisdom, clarity, effectiveness.

As you may have observed, there are similarities with the functions of the seven chakras (not surprisingly). Apart from a "measuring stick" to see at what level you are operating from yourself, I find these levels a great tool to relate with other people. If you can see that someone is operating on the level of Pleasure, there is no point in approaching this person from the level of Self-Awareness. It would be like speaking a different language, you might as well be speaking Chinese. If you want to relate to this person, you need to speak their language. Master communicators know how to do this.

You can also observe that collectively humans are in the process of evolving from the third level (Power) to the fourth level (Love). The hierarchal structures of the western societies are still based on power and control, but a growing group of people are outgrowing this level of consciousness and are starting to create new ways of living, creating a different model of society. The "old generation", the people in power, are desperately trying to hold on to their position and yielding ever more control over people, fuelled by ever more sophisticated technology. But as more and more people raise their consciousness, society will ultimately reflect this change and a new society will develop.

Something that is important to understand is the difference between consciousness and awareness. There is a lot of confusion about this, and most people (and many authors) use these words as if they have the same meaning. But there is a big difference. You may have observed that the first five levels talk about consciousness, while the last two levels talk about awareness.

Consciousness is a state of the mind. You can expand your consciousness by training your mind.

Awareness comes from no mind, it is a transcendence beyond the mind. You cannot develop awareness with mind activity. Awareness arises when you go beyond the mind.

In order to raise your consciousness, you need to break free from your habitual thinking patterns. To do that, self observation is needed, as well as an understanding of how your mind works. This is where we will start in the next chapter.

33
Your mind is a filter

Recently, neuroscientists have discovered that we receive 11 million bits of data every second. All this information comes from our senses: sights, sounds, smells, tastes, feelings. We also receive data from our body: blood pressure, temperature, condition of our organs, body functions, etc, etc. But out of all of these 11 million bits of data, only 60 are brought into our consciousness. What happens is that our subconscious mind filters what gets presented to our conscious mind, based on what we perceive as useful information. What it perceives as useful is based on our experiences, which is our past.

So quite literally *we perceive the world through a filter of our own past experiences.* This explains that when the police interrogate four witnesses of a crime, they may get four different versions of what happened.

Let me explain how this works with an example. You might have experienced this yourself at some point when you were thinking of buying a new car. Let's say you are contemplating buying a Ford Focus – all of a sudden you will see Ford Focus cars everywhere you go. Some people might think "It's synchronicity, the Universe is giving me signals that this is a good car for me", or something like that. But what is simply happening is that your subconscious mind now knows that you are interested in a Ford Focus, so any time a Ford Focus comes into view, it will present this information to your conscious mind.

It's a very clever and useful mechanism. If the subconscious mind did not filter this information, but presented all the information about cars that come into view to your conscious mind you would go nuts: "That is a blue Ford Focus. And there is a red BMW 320. And here is silver Mercedes SLK. And now a dark grey Toyota Prius, etc." ... it would be exhausting! It is not useful to receive this data all the time, so your subconscious mind filters it out for you.

I remember the first time that I travelled to Asia. When I came out of the airport at Kathmandu, Nepal, all my senses were overwhelmed. There were so many people, they were talking in a language that I did not understand, so these were all strange sounds to me. Cars beeping, cows mooing, whistles being blown, music playing out of shops... the smells were totally different, so many smells blended together: incense, food, the smell of the earth... and all the sights were new: so many colours, all the buildings that I had never seen, people looked different, colourful saris, etc... and it was so busy! After walking through Kathmandu for a few hours in the afternoon I was completely exhausted! But after a few days I was able to walk through town and feel ok. My subconscious mind had learned to filter out a lot of information and now I could function a lot better.

So the filtering process has a function: it helps us to cope with daily life and stops us from being overwhelmed with information. Remember that just because something does not get presented to your conscious mind doesn't mean that it does not get recorded. Everything gets recorded all the time!

When a baby is born there is no filter in place yet. A baby is completely open, everything is new. This is why babies get overwhelmed so easily. I remember this from when my daughter Vicky was born. When she was a week old, we ventured out for the first time with her into town. We lived in a small village in the UK at the time, which had a lovely calm green town square. We walked for a bit and went into a coffee shop for a much needed coffee. The moment we got inside, Vicky started crying. We tried to calm her down, maybe she needed a bottle? Or wanted to be held? We were desperate to be out in society for a bit after being in the house for most of the time for the last week. But whatever we tried, she did not stop crying. Then tuning into her we sensed that the energy and the noises in the place (the constant coffee machine, people chattering, background music) were too much for her. As soon as we got outside she calmed down and stopped crying.

Looking back at this it makes perfect sense. For her, being in that coffee shop was the same as it was for me to be walking in

Kathmandu that first afternoon. The only way she could communicate to us that it was too much for her, was to cry.

A baby sees the world without a filter. It sees everything for the first time. It does not label things. It just sees things as they are, with all its senses wide open. As it grows up the baby starts to lose that sensitivity – it literally starts to become desensitised. It has to, otherwise it would be overwhelmed all the time, just like Vicky was in the coffee shop. It will start to learn what is useful information (this thing gives pain when I touch it, I must remember that!) and what is not.

34
The power of beliefs

"Whether you think you can do it, or whether you think that you can't, you are right"
Henry Ford

As we grow up, our mind tries to make sense of the world. It is processing all the data that is coming in, it tries to make some sense of it. In order to do that it needs to create some order and structure. The mind creates a map of the world, a map of life. Your beliefs are that map.

Beliefs are formed by repeated experiences. Let's say that as a little child you want to play with daddy. But he needs to go to work, so he says no. In the evening when you ask him again he is tired and says no. After this happens for a third time your mind comes to the conclusion that "daddy does not want to play with me." You have formed a belief. Every time that daddy does not play with you it will reinforce that belief. At some point you will stop asking, because what's the point?

Often the mind of a child will twist things a bit, and in this case it might form the belief that "daddy does not love me" Now is this true? Maybe he had a bad day, or his mind is troubled, as he is worried that he is may lose his job.

The more a belief gets validated, the stronger it gets. This energy gets stored in your body and you will start to emit this energy out into the world, attracting events in your life that will validate this belief further. In the case of a negative belief (e.g. "men don't love me") any time that this gets triggered (you ask a man out for a date but get rejected) you get hurt again and the belief gets validated: "you see it's true, men don't love me."

Beliefs can be empowering, or they can be limiting. Once you have formed a belief it will be true for you. Of course it is, as the belief got formed based on "true" experiences for you. So no matter whether you believe that "men don't love me", or that "things always work out in the end", you are always right.

The beliefs that you have formed about life are not absolute truths. They are just truths that you have formed based on your experiences as a child. You did this in order to keep you safe, to prevent you getting hurt. If you have worked out that "daddy does not want to play with me" you will stop asking, in order not to feel the pain of rejection each time.

The good news is that now as an adult, you can examine the beliefs that you have formed, and look at whether you think they really are true or not, from the perspective of you now, as an adult. You can let go of beliefs that no longer serve you, and you can choose more positive, empowering ones.

Exercise:

What beliefs do you have about life?
Sometimes this can be quite hard to answer. A good way to find out what your beliefs are is this: just look at what is happening in your life right now. Your life right now will be an exact mirror of the beliefs you have.

35
Your imagination is real

There is no difference to your mind between what is real and what you imagine. It may sound crazy but it is really true.

You can experience this for yourself when you go to an IMAX cinema. When the screen you are watching is so big that if fills your complete field of vision, your body will take what it is seeing for real, you feel your stomach move when the person jumps off a cliff or rides a roller coaster.

What happens when you watch pornographic images? In reality you are watching small dots on a screen or paper, but the visuals that this creates and the imagination that gets stimulated, create sexual feelings and even body reactions. You are having sex in your own mind.

These are "normal" examples, but below I will share some extraordinary examples that show what we are capable of, when pushed in extreme circumstances.

One incredible story that I came across is that of an American who was captured by the Vietcong in the Vietnam war. While he was held captive in an underground cave, in order not to go crazy he started to imagine playing golf at his usual golf course at home. He spent his days imagining that he was walking around the course, playing the 18 holes. Day in day out he was playing golf in his mind, practising his drive, his putting, everything. He played on that golf course time and time again. Finally he was released after several months. Back at home he went to his golf course, and was astonished to find he played better than ever before. His handicap improved 15 points, without hitting a golf ball for a year.

Another example comes from another war. In the struggle of Indonesia to free itself from the Dutch colonists, much terrible suffering occurred. A Dutch soldier was captured and tortured by putting him in a tiny metal box that was standing on a beach in the blazing sun. He was left with no water or food. He had seen many others suffer the same fate and die from dehydration and fevers. But he was determined to survive the ordeal, so he started imagining that he was in a cool room. He focussed on this totally, to the point where he managed to control his body temperature. When he was taken out after several days not only was he still alive, but he had no burns or fever at all, though he was very weakened from the lack of food and water.

Science is interested in this as well. Several studies have been performed with athletes. One group of athletes would spend 30 minutes daily imagining to be working out in the gym, the other group would not. Both groups would spend the same time daily actually in the gym exercising. What they found was that the performance and muscle growth of the group who did the imaginary workouts was 15% better than the other group. For the brain and the body, the imaginary workout was just as real as the real one. Now they even train athletes in lucid dreaming (a dream state where you know you are dreaming) so they can train while they are dreaming. Again studies show that these athletes outperform the others who don't do this practise.

When we work with visualisations, it is actually real. I had a beautiful confirmation of this a few years ago when my daughter Vicky was about 5 years old. She was (and still is) very sensitive to energies and could often see them. Most evenings when I put her to bed I would sit next to her bed and would cleanse the energy in her room so she would sleep peacefully. I would do this silently and never told Vicky what I was doing. One night she was drifting off to sleep as I was creating a soft pink sphere all around her aura, filled with unconditional love. All of a sudden she opened her eyes and said to me: "daddy, there is a pink bubble all around me and around you as well." I smiled and asked: "and how does it feel?" She answered: "it's really nice!", then closed her eyes and fell asleep.

36
Your story

We all create a story inside our head about our life, our history. Maybe you are not even aware that you do it, but we all have a story about ourselves. When you listen to other people you can hear it very clearly. You might hear someone say something like this:

"I had a really hard childhood. My parents were always shouting at me. They preferred my sister. We never went on a holiday. They did not understand me. They just wanted me to do well at school, to get a good job and earn a lot of money. They did not love me. Nobody ever loved me. So I have always been struggling. I just don't fit into this society..."

When you start listening to other people's story, notice how often it is a negative one, a limiting one. It often keeps the person trapped in the past. How often do you hear someone say something like this:

"You know I had such a great childhood. I loved playing outside with my friends. My parents did the best that they could, even though we didn't have much money. We hardly went on holiday, but I loved going fishing at the weekends outside of town and being together like that. They wanted me to do well at school, so I could build a better life for myself."

What is your story? Is your story keeping you small, is it keeping you trapped in the past? Sometimes you "hide" the real story inside of you. But especially when you are feeling low, when you are tired and run down, the real story deep inside you will come up. In my case this used to be something like this:

*"Women don't find me attractive.
Everybody always come to me for help, but nobody is there for me when I need someone.*

I can do many things quite well, but I am not really good at anything and I never manage to get real success. I don't fit into this world."

Can you imagine the effect if you replace the limiting story in your head with an empowering one? When you look at the limiting story and examine every statement, is it really true? Can you form a more positive story? In my example it would go something like this:

Women don't find me attractive.
That comes from my childhood. Is it true? I actually don't know that. Looking back now, probably there were some girls interested in me, but I was so shy that I never approached them. The girl I was in love with for two years probably did like me but she was not allowed to date a white man. In the last few years I had a few girlfriends. In fact every time I really wanted to date a woman I usually "got" her in the end. Conclusion: this belief *"Women don't find me attractive"* is not valid anymore. I can turn it around into: *"I can be with the woman that I want."*

I never manage to get real success.
Is this true? I went from never having sailed at the age of 14, to being in the last 20 people in the selection for the Dutch Whitbread Around The World sailing team when I was 19 years old. How many people can say that? When I went into IT, I went from programming to managing large projects in the space of five years. So again, this statement is not true. I can turn this around into: *"I can achieve anything I want when I really set my mind to it"*

You can see where I am going with this. Often the story we have created about ourselves was based on experiences when we were young. Perhaps you will find that the situation has now changed, and that this story is outdated. You have a choice. What story do you want to believe? The "poor me" story, or the empowering one? You are not your past. You can shape your story anew every day. There are plenty of examples from people who have changed their story and rebuilt their life.

For example, not so long ago there was an English woman who's marriage had failed when living in Portugal. She returned to England with her one year old daughter and was living on state benefits, jobless. She felt a complete failure, was depressed and sometimes even suicidal. She decided to channel all her energy into the only thing that mattered to her, to write the children's novel she had in her head for several years. Her name was Joanne Rowling, and her "*Harry Potter*" novels became world-wide bestsellers.

You are not your story. You can change your life. The future is not an extrapolation of the past.

There is a Zen meditation from Thich Nhat Hanh that fits this beautifully:

My past is not who I am
I am not bounded by my past
My present is not who I am
I am not bounded by my present
My future is not who I am
I am not bounded by my future
I am life without limits
I am without limits
I am life
I am

Exercise

Write down the story that you tell yourself, the story that you tell to others. Be honest. Allow yourself to write the limiting story that you have in your head.

When you have finished, read your own story.
Now rewrite it. Examine every statement: is it really true? Focus on the positives that were in your life. Can you turn the statement around into a positive one? Be truthful, it needs to be a real story, not a fairy tale. Can you rewrite your story so that it empowers you?

37
You create your own reality

You will probably have heard this before: *we create our own reality*. It sounds great, and we are happy to accept this as true when things go right in our life ("I have attracted this new job into my life!") But it's much harder to accept when things don't work out. What if you cannot find a new job? What if you are still single and cannot find a new partner? "I am trying so hard – why does it not work?" you might think. You are visualising, doing daily affirmations, but nothing is happening. If we create our own reality then why is it not working? Or is it not true after all? What is going on?

What is happening is this: your energy is reflected in the world outside you. This is a deep insight that I obtained from Ho'oponopono, and it is a hard one to swallow at first: *everything that happens outside of you is a reflection of what is going on inside of you.* This means that you have total responsibility! Please read this paragraph again and let it sink in, the implications of this are huge.

What is crucial to understand is that *the sum total* of your energy creates your reality. This means: your history, your stored emotions, your beliefs, your thoughts. As we have discussed in Part Three, 90% if not 95% of your energy is stored in your subconscious. That is what determines your reality.

As a young boy I was bullied when I was in primary school. I had red hair, glasses, was the smartest boy in the class, was not joining in with the "power" games... I was different, so there plenty of ammunition for the others to pick on me. I thought it was so stupid, but of course I did feel rejected. Eventually it changed when I started playing football and through that I somehow connected with the most popular boy in the class. Later as a teenager I started becoming interested in girls. But I was shy and I didn't really know how to approach them. I was afraid of being rejected, so of course I always got rejected. The pattern of rejection was repeated with girls, as I was carrying the history of rejection through the bullying by the boys.

The energy stored in your subconscious (your history, stored emotions, beliefs) is the reason why affirmations don't work a lot of the time. It's like this: your subconscious is like a river with a strong current flowing to the right. Now with your mind you can decide that you want to swim to the left – good luck! It will be a struggle to get there. This is why it's so important to clear the emotions of the past (as discussed in part three). When you clear the past the river becomes a still pond. Now you can swim easily in any direction that you choose.

It's amazing how quickly the universe can respond to your energy. Last year I went to an amazing yoga festival in England (*Colourfest - see colourfest.co.uk*). During a dance session I met an amazing woman, our energies just completely matched and we fell in love. So I was there at the festival with my heart wide open, full of love, with a strong and a super high frequency. The next day I was at a Kirtan session (chanting). I was totally shining and a woman a bit further away looked at me. I smiled at her, and she smiled back. She was gorgeous and she started flirting with me. First I was so surprised... I don't see myself as particularly attractive, why would such a beautiful woman be interested in me? But then I realised what was happening, she was responding to my energy. Instant feedback from the Universe.

You might have had a similar experience. When you are single and craving attention from the opposite sex nothing is happening, then as soon as you find a partner and are in love, everybody notices you. Your "neediness" vibe is not attractive, your "I'm in love, I love life" vibe is very attractive. So if you want to find a partner it's very simple: fall in love with life, fall in love with yourself, and you will become the most attractive person in the world!

38
You always have a choice

"The truth will set you free, but first it will piss you off"
Gloria Steinem

One of the most dramatic moments of my life happened when I was about 12 years old. We had school swimming, which was a lot of fun, and after the lesson we always had some free time in the pool to play. I was happily swimming along when suddenly a guy climbed on my shoulders and pushed me under water. I struggled to get free but he was bigger and stronger than me. I was quickly running out of air and panicked. He was still on top of me and I thought "if he doesn't let go soon I will drown." Somehow I knew that I was wasting my energy trying to free myself, he was much stronger than me. So I stopped resisting and played dead, just trying to hold my breath. I don't know what happened next exactly, my next memory is that I was lying on the side of the pool coughing up water, with a lot of people around me. I had come very close to drowning.

It was only a few years ago, when I was going through all the major events of my life to release any stored emotions, that I looked back at this event. Only then did I realise that at the time *I made a choice* to stop fighting and let myself be overpowered. It may have well saved my life. Once the guy on top of me felt I was going limp, he had let go. This, in combination with preserving my energy, probably saved my life.

No matter what you may think, in reality you always have a choice. Whatever is happening in your life right now is because at some level you made a choice for this to be in your life. I know this might be hard to swallow for some people. Please read this again: Whatever is happening in your life right now is because at some level you are making a choice for this to be in your life.

If you are in a job that you hate, it is because you are making a choice to stay in this job.

If you are stuck in traffic each day for 1.5 hours trying to get to work, it is because you made a choice to live that far from your workplace.

If you are upset with your husband who never listens to what is really going on for you, it is because you are choosing to be with a man who treats you like this.

If you are with a partner who is abusing you, it is because you are making a choice to stay with them.

I know, it may be very hard to hear this. You might even be getting angry as you read this. The reason you are getting angry is because you know deep inside that it is true. You are not angry with me, you are angry with yourself for allowing yourself to be in the situation you are in.

"The truth will set you free – but first it will piss you off."

But it is a good thing. As painful as it may be to see the truth, it will also empower you. Once you see the situation for what it really is, which is that you are always the one who has the power to change the situation, it will empower you to take back the control of your life, to step out of the role of the victim, to take ownership, to step into your power, to take responsibility for your life.

When you look at why you are staying in these situations, you will always come to the same answer: fear. You are afraid that you will not find another job. You are afraid that you won't find another partner. You might also say that you stay in these situations because of a lack of self-love. A good question to ask yourself is this: if I loved myself completely – what choice would I make then?

You are responsible. The word "responsible" breaks down into Response and Able: you are able to respond to a situation. The most striking example of this is given by Viktor E. Frankl. He was a prominent Viennese psychiatrist before the second world war. He was arrested and ended up in the Auschwitz concentration camp.

There he observed that it was the men who comforted others and who gave away their last piece of bread who survived the longest. The sort of person the concentration camp prisoner became was the result of an inner decision and not of camp influences alone.

In his famous book *"Man's Search for Meaning"* he writes that:

"Everything can be taken from a man but one thing: the last of the human freedoms—to choose one's attitude in any given set of circumstances, to choose one's own way.

Between stimulus and response there is a space. In that space is our power to choose our response. In our response lies our growth and our freedom."

Exercise:

What is going on in your life right now. Are you choosing to stay in a situation that is not working for you?

If you loved yourself completely – what choice would you make then?

39
Intention or Inspiration

"Inspiration happens when your mind is still enough that you can hear the message that your soul is dropping into your mind"
Stef Kling

We create our own lives, we always have a choice. That is really positive, in fact it's great. So the question is: how do you create your life? Do you use your intention, or do you use your inspiration? Let me explain what I mean by this.

> Your intention comes from your mind.
> Your inspiration comes from your soul.

When you set intentions, it means that you are thinking about what you want to happen in the future. It comes from your mind, and your mind is always based on your past, your mind is always limited. Your mind will do an extrapolation of the past into the future, maybe stretch it a little and that will be your intention for the future. It will never be fresh. It will never be completely new.

Inspiration works completely differently. Your inspiration is not limited by your mind. The expression "an idea just dropped into my head" is actually a correct description of the process of inspiration. Inspiration happens when your mind is still enough so that you can hear the message that your soul is dropping into your mind.

Have you noticed that moments of inspiration come when you are not doing anything, when your mind is quiet? It often happens whilst having a shower, or just after you wake up. It happens when you are daydreaming. It even happens in your dreams. The 3M company (they invented the yellow post-it notes) recognises this principle and encourage their staff to take regular naps, as they know that the creative impulse often happens after a nap when the mind is rested.

Music often comes from pure inspiration. Mozart said that the music he composed "would just appear in my head, I just wrote it down on paper." The band REM wrote their biggest hit "Losing my religion" in just 10 minutes. Their singer and songwriter Michael Stipe said that "the song just seemed to be there in the ether, all I had to do was to write it down."

There was a time when I was trying to create music on my computer using a synthesizer (though I never got very far as I can't play piano). Several times during this period it happened that I would wake up with a complete song in my head. Other times when I was having a shower, a melody would come to me out of nowhere.

Years later I had a crazy experience. One night I had a dream and in this dream I was driving in my car. I put on the new CD from one of my favourite bands, Nightwish. The first songs were nice, but track 3 and 4 were totally amazing! It was better than anything they had ever done before. When these tracks finished I listened to them again. I was blown away, I totally loved it! Then I woke up. I could still hear these two songs in my head, from start to finish. But this was new music, the CD that I listened to in my dream did not exist. I so wished that I could write down music – I could have written the complete score of all the parts of these songs and then give it to the band.

But it gets even weirder. About one and a half year later the singer from that band, Tarja, released a new solo album. When I listened to that CD I instantly loved the middle part of one song, it was as if I knew it already. Then I realised that this was a part of the song that I heard in that dream! It was a bit different from how I heard it, but it definitely had the same melody and orchestration.

Inspiration allows for something completely new to arrive. Something completely fresh, totally unlimited. How do you think that someone like Tesla got his ideas? Do you really think that his mind just thought how to create unlimited free energy?

"*The Secret*", and lots of other books about the Law of Attraction, mainly talk about working with your intention. You use the power of your mind: visualising, doing affirmations etc, to attract into your life what you want to get. That is all valid, but don't let yourself be limited by what your mind can think of. Allow your soul to be in charge and create an unlimited life for yourself.

Free will or free won't

Now some people might say "It's all very nice to act on inspiration - but when you do this, what about free will? Are you not handing your life over to God (the Universe)?"

When you have an inspiration, when an idea drops into your head, you have a choice. You can decide that you will act on it (free will), or you can decide that you won't act on it (free won't). The choice is yours.

You might have had the experience in your life that you had an inspiration, but you didn't follow up on it. Then some time later you find that someone else had the same idea and implemented it. If you won't follow up on the idea, often the universe will find another recipient who will listen. And that is totally fine, you really do have free will. Now you might wonder: "If I had this idea, was I not supposed to act on it?" This leads into another discussion, about Fate and Destiny...

Exercise:

Think about your own life: when did you create things using your intention? Have there been times when you felt inspired? Did you follow that inspiration? Can you feel or see a difference between the two?

40
Fate and Destiny

There is a lot of confusion around fate and destiny. Is our life pre-destined? Are events that are happening in your life just your fate? People often use the terms fate and destiny for the same thing, for example when someone says: "you will meet your fate at the end of your life." But fate and destiny are two different things. The simplest way that I can put it is like this:

> Fate is the card you were dealt in life.
> Destiny is where you are meant to end up in your life, what you are meant to do with those cards.

It is your fate that you were born in England, that you have blue eyes and blonde hair, that you are an attractive woman. It is your fate that your parents split up when you were five, that you had an aggressive father, that your family had to flee Syria and build a new life in Germany. Fate is the circumstances that happen in your life.

You cannot change fate. You cannot change the family that you grew up in. When your father dies you cannot bring him back to life. When your country turns into a war zone, there is nothing you can do about it. Sometimes your life seems to flow so well, everything is going right and then - boom! Life intervenes and completely throws your life upside down.

When I was young, my big dream was to compete in what is now known as the Volvo Ocean Race – a yacht race sailing around the world, that is held every four years. It is the formula one of ocean racing. I got this dream after I saw a documentary on TV when I was 11 years old, about the Dutch yacht "Flyer" winning the 1977/78 edition of the Whitbread Around The World Race (as it was called then). Something deep inside me was stirred, I just knew that this was what I wanted to do in life. No "normal life" for me – I was going to race around the world! A few years later (I was only 19 years old) I entered the selection process to become a crew member of the Dutch yacht "Equity & Law II." There were 800 applicants for just 10 positions in the team. Despite being so young I managed to get into the last 20. Although I was not selected (too young, not enough life experience) I did sail with the team for six months. I had a fantastic time and gained invaluable experience; my dream was becoming a reality, it was within reach. Four years later it was the start of the next campaign. This time I was on a short-list of 20 people. From these 20 people the final crew of 10 people would be chosen. I knew that one of the biggest deciding factors was personality, and I already knew that this was perhaps my biggest asset. All I had to do was to develop my boat handling skills in the campaign. I was totally prepared to quit my job once the new boat was built and go for it. This was my time, this was going to be my race around the world.

Then one evening in December I got a phone call from Gideon, the skipper. "Stef, I am afraid I have bad news" he said. "Our main sponsor just informed me that they have to withdraw. They are having to make 2000 people redundant, and although they feel sponsoring the campaign would still be a good marketing and PR investment, the board has decided that they cannot justify spending millions on a yacht race whilst ending the employment for so many people"... It was a bombshell. We were just about to start building the new boat. There was not enough time to find a new sponsor and the whole campaign fell apart. For the first time there was no Dutch entry in the race. When I got that phone call I knew immediately that this was the end of my dream. We lost the momentum in Holland. Every edition was getting more and more professional, and crews were becoming more international. In four years time it would be very hard to secure a place in the Dutch team, if there even would be a Dutch entry next time. It was my fate that there was no Dutch entry just when I was totally ready...

Looking back now it is easy to see that it was not my destiny to become a professional sailor, spending my life racing yachts around the oceans of the world. At the time it was an incredible blow. I had been living for this for such a long time. This race was in my mind, in my dreams, every day for 8 years. Soon after I got the news, I decided to stop yacht racing and I fell into a black hole. Life had lost its purpose, or so it seemed at the time. It took me a few years to get over it. I threw myself into building a career, got a girlfriend, bought and renovated a house, was having a "normal" life, but then destiny knocked on my door...

So what is destiny? Your destiny is where you are heading. You could look at it in this way: your life is like a river flowing down from the mountain; it is destined to reach the sea. Sometimes the river will turn left, sometimes it will turn right. Sometimes it seems to go backwards, but it will always find a way to get where it is destined to go. The river doesn't have a map, it doesn't flow down in one straight line to the ocean. When there is an obstacle in it's path, it will just change course and flow around it. But the pull towards the ocean is always there and inevitably it will reach it's final destination.

It is the same for us. We don't get a map of our life, we don't walk in a straight line to our final destination. We twist and we turn just like the river does. Yes, we have free will. We can decide to turn left, even if all the signs seem to suggest we should go right. But if we are destined to end up somewhere on the right side, life will take us there. That is what destiny does, it is always calling us, whispering to us, guiding us home. And if we don't listen, then sometimes life intervenes and shakes us up.

In my case, suddenly my dream of racing around the world got shattered. But although it was a massive blow, at least it was relatively harmless. Some people get cancer as an ultimate wake up call.

The art of life is to listen to your soul. The more you can do this, the more you can be aligned, the more your life will flow towards the ocean. This does not mean that life will be easy and full of bliss - sometimes the direct path can also throw up the biggest obstacles. But when you live your life from this place, when there is an alignment between your soul, mind, heart and actions, then you will be in perfect balance and you will be able to sail with the currents of life. Life will become a beautiful adventure, rather than an obstacle course.

41
Karma

I have spoken about Fate and Destiny and a concept that is closely related to that is Karma. So what is Karma, is it some sort of revenge from the Gods? A cosmic punishment if you do bad things? Or simply the law of cause and effect: what comes around goes around?

I have seen lovely spiritual people say things like this: "These people in Ethiopia are poor and half starving to death, yes it is terrible, but you know, it is their karma." What nonsense!

Some Buddhists use Karma in a way where they believe that if you earn enough merit in this life, you will have a better life next time. As much as I value the Buddhist teachings, this does not sit right with me. It is still a form of fear, of reward and punishment: "if I am a good person in this life I will get rewarded in my next life", which then by default means that if I am not good in this life, I will not get a good next life. Who decides what is good and not good? And if I just score enough points, earn enough merit, I will get enlightened?

I am going to make a case here to completely scrap the whole concept of Karma. For one, nobody can be really sure how it works. Secondly, it is used a lot to justify a certain situation: "it's his karma, so he will have to deal with it." It is a convenient "truth" that gives you permission not to do anything about it. Thirdly, it just distracts from the situation. When you are in a certain situation, it doesn't matter if it was a reward or a punishment, if it was your karma.

When this guy jumped on my neck in the swimming pool and nearly drowned me, did it matter if it was my Karma or not?
When Hitler gassed millions of Jews, was it the Karma of the Jewish people?
When a child is born starving in Ethiopia, is it their Karma? Have they been bad in a past life?

There may well be a thing like Karma, cause and effect. The problem is that we think that we understand how this works. But that understanding comes from our ego, from the limited vision of our mind. If there is one thing that I have learned from all the guide writings I have done for people over the last twenty years, then it is this: we know nothing. We perceive life from a very limited perspective.

Does it matter whether the situation that you are in is karmic or not? In the end, what matters is only this: what are you going to do about it.

42
Your mind is a beast

"If you correct your mind, the rest of your life will fall into place"
Lao Tzu

When you start to observe your own mind, there is only one conclusion possible: your mind is a beast. There is no "off" button, it's always busy! Have you ever realised what your mind is actually doing all the time? When you start observing your thoughts, you will see that they fit into just a few categories.

The first favourite activity of your mind is to go over the past. Sometimes your mind is replaying nice memories. But what tends to happen is that your mind is replaying painful memories over and over again. It's a bit like watching a horror movie time and time again, it's crazy. Especially if you did something wrong or made a mistake, your mind will go over the situation time and time again, judging yourself, blaming yourself. You are your own worst enemy.

But here is a strange phenomenon: after some time has gone by, the past is made to look better, more pleasant than it was. We tend to forget the bad stuff and remember the good bits. You may have noticed this yourself. This is why people often say that "when I was young things were better." It's not that things were better then, or more exciting. There were just as many boring, uninteresting days as now, only they get filtered out. And the unpleasant memories get suppressed after some time, so it seems that it was better. This is why people often say that "time heals all wounds." This is a fallacy. Just because lots of people say something, it does not mean that it is true. Time does not heal wounds, the wounds get pushed into the sub-conscious.

Let's move on to the second favourite mind activity: Thinking of the future. This we can summarise in two words: Hopes and Fears. We are hoping for something to happen: dreaming that he will fall in love with you, finally getting pregnant, that my book will become a bestseller. Or we are in fear of what might happen: what if he doesn't like me? Now we are creating a horror movie that hasn't even happened yet. The fact is that most of these fears will never happen. So why spend all that mind energy thinking about it? And should it happen, then there is another wisdom that is applicable: The fear of pain is worse than the pain itself. So if you catch yourself going into fear of the future: stop. You are wasting your energy, focus your mind on something else, come back to the now.

The third mind activity is this: Your mind is judging what is happening now. There is this constant running commentary in your head, just like a sports commentator: "oh she looks pretty", "lot's of cars on the road today", "that is a Toyota", "gosh he gained weight", "what tree is that, oh I think it's a beech", "oh there is a rose growing there, pretty", etc, etc. We are just like a toddler who is pointing and naming everything they see, only we do it silently in our head!

Then there is the last category: solving a practical problem. For example you are working out what bus to take to London, and determining what time you need to be at the bus station. This is actually the only useful purpose of your mind, it's what it was built for: solving problems. It's also why your mind tends to go over problems in the past and worries over possible problems in the future. Your mind just loves problems. So much so, that often if there is no problem it will create one (but more on that later).

So that is the top four of mind activities:
- going over the past
- thinking of the future
- giving a running commentary
- solving a problem

Have a go and observe for yourself if what I'm saying is right or not. It's a fun game.

Perhaps by now you will agree that your mind is a beast. So what can we do about it? Can we tame the beast? How? The answer is yes, and the way how is mindfulness, which is essentially being totally in the now.

Being in the now

Let me explain this principle with an example from my own life. My daughter Vicky loved jumping on the trampoline in the garden. Often she would ask: *"daddy can you come and jump with me?"* Often I would say no, as life was busy and there was always something to do in the house and for my work. But she was relentless and so at some point I would usually give in. Often when I was on the trampoline with her I was not really there, I was resenting having to jump with her, because I had all these things to do: I needed to tidy up the kitchen, make dinner, send that email... One day I realised what I was doing. The fact was that the moment that I stepped on the trampoline, *I* made that choice. Ok, Vicky pestered me for 30 minutes perhaps, but it was *me* who chose to go on that trampoline. So if I decided to go on the trampoline, I might as well enjoy it! So the next time I went on I let go of all the things on my mind and just focussed on Vicky and on enjoying being on the trampoline. I had a great time!

It's a very simple example, but you can apply this principle to everything that you do in your life. When you do something, give it 100% of your attention. In this way, doing the dishes can become a meditation. But what you are doing is much more that just doing the dishes. By not allowing your mind to drift off, you are de-programming your mind. You are training your mind to stop wandering off in the past or the future, to concentrate on the now, to be silent.

43
Luxury problems

"Have you noticed that whenever there is a problem, you are there?"
Dr. Hew Len

"It's not the problem that's the problem. It's your perception of the problem that's the problem"
Captain Jack Sparrow

It often seems that our life is full of problems. For some people their whole life is just one big problem, they go from one problem to the next. You can recognise who these people are: they are the ones with wrinkles, looking old, tired, unhealthy, stressed...

But when is a problem a problem? Often a problem is only a problem if you make it one. One of my favourite sayings from Dr Hew Len is this: *"Have you noticed that whenever there is a problem, you are there?"*

"My wife didn't want to have sex with me tonight." Is that a problem?
"My daughter wants me to jump on the trampoline with her, but I have so many other things to do." Is that a problem?
"I have to go to work, doing a job I don't like, in order to earn money to pay my rent." Is that a problem?
"I put on weight again, eating too many cakes." Is that a problem?

Your mind is a beast. It just loves solving problems, that is what it was made for. So if there is no problem it will create one. Now it has something to do, now it can be busy thinking about it and trying to find a solution for it. Your mind loves to be busy all the time!

It's actually quite funny when you start to look at it from a distance. When you start observing your problems, you will find that most of the time your problems are not real problems at all.

Luxury problems

I often say to my clients: *"There are problems and there are luxury problems."* What I mean by this is that most of the things that we perceive as problems are not real problems at all. They are what I call Luxury Problems.

We are blessed to live in a society where there are not many real problems. We all get to eat reasonably well, we all have a decent shelter, decent clothes, we are warm and dry. Most of our basic needs are met. So what do I mean with "Luxury Problems?" I will explain this with an example.

A friend of mine came to me one evening totally stressed out and asked me for advice: "I have a problem. I don't know which house to buy, this one or that one." This really was a big problem for her. Now she is a total super woman who manages to juggle a senior manager position in a hospital, run a household, raise two teenagers (all this whilst being a single parent), renovate the house, grow her own food, and she makes it all look easy. But this situation about the new house completely floored her. For a week she had hardly been able to sleep, it was constantly on her mind. What should she do? After I had listened to her, I pointed out that I would love to have her problem! She looked at me surprised, so I explained the concept of Luxury Problems to her. She totally got it, a weight lifted from her shoulders and we had a good laugh about it.

Once you can see that the problem in your life is actually a luxury problem, it changes everything. You can relax, you start to see things more clearly, you can think straight again. Somehow the solution to the problem will present itself to you much more easily.

> *"We can't solve problems by using the same kind of thinking we used when we created them"* - Albert Einstein

Look at these situations again and see for yourself if they are a problem or a luxury problem:

"My wife didn't want to have sex with me tonight."

"My daughter wants me to jump on the trampoline with her, but I have so many other things to do."
"I have to go to work, doing a job I don't like, in order to earn money to pay my rent."
"I put on weight again, eating too many cakes."

You get the idea. When you start looking at problems in this way, you will find that most things that we make into a problem are not real problems, but luxury problems. When we recognise this, it is the first step to disidentify from it. It makes it lighter somehow.

When you look back in half a year's time at the problem you are dealing with today, you will most likely laugh at it. So if that is the case, then why not try to laugh at it now?

Dealing with problems

When you look into it, you will find that problems mostly fall into one of three categories:

- Having to making a decision (*"do I buy this house or that one"*)
- Regretting a choice that we made (*"I wish that I rented that house near the forest"*)
- Wanting things to be different than they are (*"my wife didn't want to have sex with me tonight"*)

Let's look a bit more into each of these scenario's and find out how we can deal with these problems.

Having to making a decision:
This is often not a real problem, but a luxury problem. We need to make a decision, so we need to use all our capabilities (logical mind, intuition and feeling) to try to make the best possible choice for us. Be glad that life is giving you a choice, how wonderful is that!

A little advice about making a choice (this goes back from my days in management). Let's say that you need to make a choice and there are three options: A, B and C. Often when you look at the pros and cons, there will be one option that is clearly not favourable (let's say option C). So take that one off the table. Now the choice is just between option A or B. Sometimes when you look at these options, one is more favourable. So that solves the problem. Sometimes no matter how long you look at the situation, both options look equally valid. In that case it is simple: just pick one! If they both look equally attractive, then it doesn't matter which one you take. Personally in this case I would go with my gut feeling, or intuition.

The last and perhaps the most difficult situation, is when your mind says one thing (option A) and your heart something else (option B). This is where it gets interesting, especially when it is a big decision. Do you follow your mind or your heart? A lot of us were taught to be "sensible" and use our mind: "you have to do what is right", especially when it is a big decision. I cannot tell you what is right or wrong, sometimes you will follow your mind, sometimes your heart. But here is one question that has helped me many times: are you making the choice out of fear, or out of love? There is more on that in a later chapter.

Regretting a choice that you made:
"I wish that I rented that house near the forest." This is actually not a problem today at all. You made a choice in the past, you cannot change that now. All you can do is to accept it and move on. This may sound too easy, but it is very profound. Perhaps you can change the situation, but there is no point in going over the past and beating yourself up about it. Maybe in hindsight, with the information that you have now, you can see that it would have been better to take a different decision, but at the time you did not have that information. *You did the best that you could at that time.* When you think about it logically, the only thing that you can do is to accept the current situation and move on.

We want things to be different than they are:
"My wife didn't want to have sex with me tonight. I wish that I was rich. I wish that I did not have to go to work. I wish that my ex-wife did not leave me." Well, we can wish all we want, but the fact is that the situation is how it is. The only thing you can do is to accept the reality and move on. It is madness to waste your energy on wishing that things are different from what they are. There is more on this in the next chapter.

Flip it

Here is another great way to deal with problems: Flip it around and think about all the things for which you are grateful.

Got a parking ticket? Be grateful that you even have a car. Be grateful that you're going to be able to help pay for someone's wages.

Did you stub your toe? Be grateful that you have a toe to stub, that you have such a great life that this is probably the worst thing that will happen to you today.

Are the kids being challenging? Be grateful that they are healthy enough to make so much noise and honour them for the growth that you both experience together.

Whatever it is that is happening in your life, remember that you can always choose your optimal response. Remember the wisdom from Victor Frankl in the concentration camp.

Conclusion

Why do I talk about problems so much? I do this because a LOT of your mental energy is spent on dealing with problems. So in a way this is perhaps one of the most important chapters of this book. If you can learn how to deal with problems and reduce the impact they have on your mind, and therefore on your life, you will make a huge step towards living lighter. You are taming the beast. So I invite you to test out the principles that I have described in this chapter in real life situations. Read this chapter again when a problem comes up in your life. See if these principles work for you. When you learn to master your problems, you learn to master your life.

44
Acceptance

"When there is true acceptance, suffering ends"
Buddha

A lot of our pain is caused by resisting what is. I don't mean physical pain, like when you stub your toe against a chair, but emotional pain. When we want things to be different than they are, we create suffering for ourselves. Here is an example that I'm sure we all have experienced in our life at one point.

Let's say that I meet a girl. She is beautiful, her energy is amazing, the way that she moves, the way that her eyes shine with light, I love everything about her. I fall madly in love with her, I want to be with this girl, I want her to love me. Initially I feel great, I'm in love and life is wonderful, everything seems to have more colour. I float through the days thinking of her, my heart is open and love is flowing out of it. But slowly I realise that despite all my efforts to win her over, it's not happening, her response is not how I want it to be. For some time I remain blind to the truth, because I don't want to see it. So I keep trying and trying. But slowly I realise that she is not in love with me. Now the pain starts and it hurts like hell.

Why am I hurting? Because I am not accepting what is. I want it to be different, I want her to love me. I am resisting what is, I am resisting the truth. The truth is that she does not love me. The moment when I fully accept that, I can let her go and move on. But as long as I don't accept it, as long as I keep wanting her and keep hoping, I will keep myself locked in pain. Only when I can accept the truth, will my mind stops wanting things to be different. When there is true acceptance suffering ends.

You wake up and it's raining, but you want it to be sunny. You get into a bad mood, you are suffering.

Your favourite football team has lost the final and you feel miserable next day. You are suffering.

After days of deliberation you finally decide to buy that beautiful dress that you've seen, but when you get to the shop they sold the last one yesterday. You are gutted, you are suffering.

These are every day examples, and it is easy to overcome these little obstacles in life. But they show the mechanics of suffering: the moment when you accept the situation, you can let go and suffering ends. Here is a real story from my life that shows how powerful acceptance can be when big things happen in life.

One time my mum had a cold. She had it for a while and it didn't want to go away, so she went to her GP. He gave her antibiotics, after which her throat started swelling up. She often had allergic reactions to medicine, so she didn't think too much about it. When she went back to the GP he sent her for a scan to the Hospital, just to be sure that nothing serious was going on. When the first results came back she was told that she had a very late stage of lung cancer. She was terminally ill.

It was a total shock. Apart from having this cough she had been feeling fine, a bit more tired than normal perhaps. Now she was told that she had about three months left to live. We were all devastated by the news. We were in shock. What would happen? How soon? How bad would it get? She decided to undergo chemotherapy, as it might give her another year to live. There was a lot of pain, a lot of fear, a lot of suffering. And not only for my mum. What about my dad? He was only 53, just like my mum. They had a very close and really loving and harmonious relationship, they always did everything together. How would he cope when my mum died?

When this happened (in 1997) I had just learned to communicate with spirit guides using automatic writing (this is the same process that Neale Donald Walsh used to write his "*Conversations with God*" books). My mum asked me if I could ask her guides why this was happening. They said the following:

Guides: "Your mum is allowed to go home."

Me: Allowed to go home? She is dying! Why?
Guides:" She created a loving marriage, she raised your sister and you, she has always been there for people. She lived a life of love. She did what she came here to do. So she is allowed to go home."
Me: Maybe for her that is ok, but what about my dad?
Guides: "Your dad will be ok. This whole experience will open him spiritually, and he will bring out this spirituality in his paintings. That would never happen if he remained with your mum."

When I read this message to my parents something incredible happened. The words from the guides went straight into my mum's heart, she could feel the truth of it. She knew that this was exactly how it was. And right there in that moment she totally accepted that she was dying. In that moment her suffering went. The same thing happened for my dad, he could feel the truth of what they said about him. He was starting to open spiritually and he knew that somehow he needed to go through this process alone. He could feel the truth about my mum. He too, totally accepted what was happening.

It was the most incredible transformation that I have ever witnessed. One moment we were all in pain, and a minute later we were all in a state of love. For all of us a deep acceptance had happened and the pain was lifted. Instead, we were lifted into a state of pure love. We could see the divine miracle of it all, somehow we could see the fabric of life for a brief moment. And we knew that everything was perfect exactly as it was. We fell in love with life, and my mother especially went into a place where she was completely in the now. She was grateful for every day that she still had together with my dad.

This has been one of the biggest lessons in my life. I was shown in the most powerful way that when there is true acceptance, suffering ends. And that acceptance can happen in just one moment.

45
Forgiveness

"We often hold a grudge because we don't want to let the other person off the hook. But who's really hooked: the one who's moved on, or the one who's holding on?"
Lori Deschene

"Forgiveness is mending a broken fragment of our heart so that we can love again"
Rachel Bell

We all get hurt in life by another person. When you don't forgive, you keep anger or even hate inside of you. By forgiving the other person, you set yourself free. When you don't forgive, you are hurting yourself. You are keeping an energetic link with that person - you are not free and they are not free. A lot of people think that forgiveness is about the other person, that you are doing it for them. But you forgive mostly for yourself. When you forgive, you let the pain and the anger go, you set yourself free and you set the other person free in the process too.

How can you do this? How can you forgive someone who has hurt you, sometimes even intentionally? There is a Zen parable (author unknown) that shows you how:

If your past was my past
If your pain was my pain
If your experiences were my experiences
If your level of consciousness was my level of consciousness
Then I would do exactly the same

Forgiveness is a key part of your healing process. When you forgive you become lighter. The practice of forgiveness is a part of emptiness.

A couple of years ago, I decided to break up with my girlfriend at the time. She was totally in love with me, but I soon felt that she was not the one for me. She was hurt and she got angry, or rather, she got furious. She started sending me text messages, calling me all kinds of things, telling me that she would destroy me, destroy my reputation, etc. etc. I asked her to stop, but the text messages kept coming, so I switched off my phone. When I turned it back on the next morning, the text messages that were queued started coming in. There were over a hundred messages! She had spent hours sending one message after another. Messages were still flooding in, but I did not respond. I could feel her anger coming at me, it was pretty severe. The whole morning I was consciously transmuting the anger coming at me into love. Then finally the texts stopped. I knew that she was just hurting and that this was her painbody talking to me. I knew that her anger must have been about much more than just me breaking up with her. So I forgave her. Later she apologised and we remained friends.

Whatever is happening in your life, you can use it to practice mastery. In the movie *"Human"* by Yann Arthus-Bertrand, there is an incredible powerful interview with a prisoner. He tells his history, how he used to be beaten up by this father. "I did it because I love you", his father would say. He ended up in prison with a life sentence for murdering a woman and her child. He tells how he learned about what love really is, from the mother of the woman that he had murdered. She would visit him in prison and talk to him, listen to him. She looked past what he did, she wanted to understand how he came to murder her daughter and grandchild. She forgave him and gave him love.

If the mother of a child is able to forgive his murderer, it means that it must be possible for you to forgive the person who has hurt you.

Forgiving yourself

Sometimes the hardest things to do is to forgive yourself. We can be our own worst enemy, always judging ourselves. How can you forgive yourself when you have made a terrible choice, and life has fallen apart as a result of it? The answer is: you did the best that you could at that time.

Almost all people are inherently good. We want to do well, for ourselves and for others. We don't do things to deliberately harm other people, or to harm ourselves. When we make certain choices, when we take certain actions, it is because at that time we believe that this is the right thing to do. It is so easy to see in hindsight that you should have made a different choice. Remember the Zen wisdom:

If your experiences were my experiences,
If your level of consciousness was my level of consciousness...

Now, you have different experiences than when you made that decision. Your consciousness has changed. You have seen the outcome of your decisions. It's so easy to tell yourself now that you should have done something different. But: you did the best that you could at that time. This insight is where forgiveness comes from. This is where self love comes from.

Exercise:

Are you holding anger inside? Who are you still angry with? Can you forgive them?

Do you still harbour anger or regret about something you did in the past? Can you forgive yourself?

46
Gratitude

"When you are grateful, when you can see what you have, you unlock blessings to flow in your life"
Suze Orman

I have found that the practice of gratitude is one of the quickest ways to raise my frequency. It is the exact opposite of complaining about your life, it is focussing your attention on the good things in your life, the things that you are grateful for. Gratitude is bliss.

Whatever you give your attention and energy to grows, so by focussing on the good things in life, you are feeding exactly that. When you practice gratitude, you are giving the Universe feedback on what you want more of in life. And it is so simple! Here are a few ways in which you can practice gratitude:

Before you go to sleep:
When you lie in bed, or when you sit in the bath before bedtime, think of ten things from your day that you are grateful for. They don't have to be big things, it can be the little things that matter. For example, I am grateful for:
- The fact that my body is healthy
- The joy that my dogs greets me with in the morning, or every time when I come back home
- The feeling of the warm sunshine on my face when I had lunch outside
- The company and the hugs of a friend in the evening
- The fact that I have a safe warm house.

When you feel that your energy is low, when you feel stuck, or when your mind is obsessed about a certain problem, you can do the same exercise. Take some time to think of ten things that you are grateful for, and you will see that it changes your energy. You will raise your frequency, and in doing so you will get unstuck. You will find that your mind breaks out of a negative pattern of thinking and you can approach a problem from a different angle.

Carrying a gratitude stone:
Another thing that you can do is to select a special stone (it can be any stone, it doesn't have to be a crystal) and put it in your pocket. Any time that you touch that stone, think of a thing that you are grateful for. In the movie *"The Secret"* they told the story of a man whose son was dying from a rare disease. He heard about gratitude and got a gratitude stone for his whole family. A few months later his son had completely healed. That is how powerful gratitude can be.

47
We know nothing

"If you want to make God laugh, tell him about your plans"
Woody Allen

By the time we have become adults, we think that we understand life, that we know how things work. We think that we can plan our life and be in control. But it's an illusion. In reality we know nothing.

It is as if we are going through life walking backwards. The only thing that we can see is the past, and based on the path we have walked so far we are deciding where to go next. But we cannot see the road that is ahead of us, we cannot see into the future. We may think that we are in control of our life, but we don't know where the next bend in the road is, or whether we will fall off a cliff in the next few steps. All we can do is to make a best guess of where we think the road will go next.

When I was studying in Holland, some of my friends were talking about wanting to work and live abroad. I always thought: "not for me, I am happy here, I will stay in Holland." Twelve years later I was living in Rotterdam, in a small but beautiful house just outside town along a canal, in the middle of nature. I worked for a Management Consultancy company, doing a job that I loved and that gave me a lot of freedom. I had a company car, a good income and was financially secure. At that point in time I would have laughed if someone had told me that six months later I would be living in England. But that is exactly what happened. Sometimes life turns a corner when you least expect it. We know nothing.

Another thing that is important to realise, is that your understanding of life is based on the experiences that you have had in your life so far. You literally see life through the filter of your past experiences. If you were born in a rich upper class family who owns a large estate and several companies, your view of life will be vastly different from someone who grew up in a rough neighbourhood with parents that are unemployed. Based on your experiences you might see a certain event as a problem, whereas someone else might see the same event as an opportunity. You might label something as bad, while someone else might label it as something good. It is all a matter of perspective. We tend to look at things from our mind, and our mind is always based on our past experiences. It's good to remind ourselves that we only have a narrow vision, a bit like a horse with blinkers. We don't see the whole picture. We know nothing.

There is a beautiful Zen story that I love:

There was an old farmer who had worked his crops for many years. One day his horse ran away. Upon hearing the news, his neighbours came to visit. "Such bad luck" they said sympathetically. "Maybe", the farmer replied.

The next morning the horse returned, bringing with it seven other wild horses. "How lucky!" the neighbours exclaimed. "Maybe", replied the old man.

The following day, the farmer's son tried to ride one of the untamed horses, was thrown off and broke his leg. "How awful", the neighbours said, "It looks like your luck has turned for the worse again." "Maybe", answered the farmer.

The next day, military officials came to the village to draft young men into the army. Seeing that the son's leg was broken, they passed him by. The neighbours congratulated the farmer on how well things had turned out. "Maybe", said the farmer.

One of the most dramatic examples that I have seen comes from my own life. In a previous chapter I told the story about my mum, how she was diagnosed as terminally ill with cancer. She decided to undergo chemotherapy, as it would buy her some time, maybe she could live another year or two. But the chemo was horrible and destroyed her body. I wrote with my guides about this:

Me: Why did she need to get cancer? The chemotherapy is destroying her body, this is a horrible way to die!
Guides: "It is an honour to die this way. It will be a very conscious process. She has always been giving, now she will learn to receive. You will help her to remove her block to spirituality. That is your gift to her. And her death, and her process of dying will be an inspiration for many, it will show that dying can be a beautiful process."

I was surprised by the totally different perspective that the guides had on this: "*she is allowed to go home... It is an honour to die this way...*" Things turned out exactly as the guides said. It really taught me that we don't see the whole picture. The soul's perspective is totally different from our mind's ego perspective, it really is a much wider view than the narrow vision of our mind.

So next time you are in a situation and you think it's a problem – remember that it is only your mind that is making it into a problem. Is it a problem? Or a blessing in disguise? Who knows... we know nothing. Allow for a much bigger picture than the narrow vision of your mind.

48
Fear

"There is nothing to fear but fear itself"
Franklin D. Roosevelt

"The fear of pain is worse than the pain itself"
Unknown

What is Fear? This may seem like a strange question, because we all know fear. But do you understand fear? When you start observing fear you will soon come to realise that there are two types:
- Acute fear; and
- Fear of the future

The first fear, acute fear, is what I call "fear of the tiger." This is the fear that you feel when you are confronted with a dangerous situation: there is a tiger standing in front of you, your house is on fire. This fear is an instinctive reaction, it is immediate, there is no thinking involved. This fear is useful, as it triggers the "fight or flight" response, which gives us the energy that is needed to deal with the situation at hand.

The second fear is what I call "fear of the future." This is a very different kind of fear. This fear comes from the mind, it comes from thinking about a possible future situation that we don't want to happen. You are afraid that you will fail the exam, that your partner will leave you, that you won't find a new job. How will you find money to buy the new car that you need?

There is a lot of conditioning around fear: "don't be afraid", "a real man should not be scared of anything" etc, but fear in itself is a positive mechanism. It wants to keep us safe, it wants to prevent us from getting hurt; either from the tiger, or by a situation in the future. Acute fear is always valid. However, fear of the future is mostly not useful. It uses up a lot your (mental) energy, and it lowers your frequency dramatically. Fear limits our capacity to see things clearly, to think straight, and in extreme cases it can completely paralyse you.

Action cures Fear

So how do you deal with fear? There is only one solution: take action! It is like the saying: "feel the fear and do it anyway." The more you procrastinate, the more time you spend worrying about the situation, the more energy you lose. Worrying about the future will not help you. The only thing that will help you is to take action. The more action you take, the better you will feel. Your frequency will start to go up. You are feeling the fear, but you don't let it control you. You are stepping into your power.

This may sound too easy perhaps, but it really is this simple. Actually it is very profound. But the only way to realise this is through personal experience. Think back to past situations in your life, how did you overcome a fearful situation? Try to apply this principle in your life. The more you practise this, the more you will be able to control your fears about the future. Your fears will not have so much control over you any more, the fear will shrink smaller and smaller.

You can decide to completely let go of fear

This may sound farfetched, so let me explain this with a personal example. When I separated from my wife Leona, the timing could have not been worse. I just finished a contract role and had no income. Leona and I were on very good terms and she was supportive, however she was spending a lot of her time working in the Czech Republic and therefore it was mostly me looking after our daughter in England. I had to find a new place to live, I had no money, I had no income. We just ended our marriage and my family was in Holland. How was I supposed to look after my daughter? How could I find a job whilst being there for her? I totally went into fear. It was so bad that when I used to wake up in the morning and came to my senses, reality would hit and the fear would hit my stomach like this huge ball of heavy energy. It was the most difficult period of my life, it was dreadful. But it also taught me a lot.

I had to take action. I had to get myself out of this situation somehow. I moved into a room (together with Vicky) that a friend offered us in her house. Somehow I managed to create a job that allowed me to work from home with flexible hours so I could be there for Vicky when she came out of school. I found a mobile home to live in (Vicky loved it, it felt like a holiday to her). Then finally after six months I could move into a family house again.

When I looked back at this time, I could see that the intense suffering that I had experienced was completely created by my own mind, by my fears. The fear of pain (the future) was much worse than the pain (the actual situation) itself. My situation might have been uncomfortable, but I was ok. Somehow I always got what I needed. I decided that if I could get through this, I could get through anything. I decided never to be afraid again.

49
Love

"If you love somebody, set them free"
Sting

What is Love? This is actually a very difficult question to answer. Most songs and movies are about love, we all instinctively know what love is, or so we think, but to put it into words is almost impossible. In a way it is easier to say what love is not.

Love is the absence of judgement

It seems that we are always judging: "look at that woman, she should lose weight ", "look at that crooked tree", or "what a scruffy dog, it's so ugly." Can a dog be ugly? Can a tree be ugly? Can a person be ugly? Who decides if someone is beautiful or not? Who decides if you wear nice clothes or not? One year you should wear long skirts and have low heels to look good, the next year you should wear short skirts and high heels to look good. It's ridiculous!

How much energy are you wasting with your continuous judging? The reason we judge other people is to feel better about ourselves. If you loved yourself completely you would have no need to judge anybody. If you are the Buddha then every person, every tree, every dog becomes beautiful. So you can say that love is the absence of judgement.

Most of all you are continuously judging yourself. You are always trying to live up to some standard. There are standards set by your parents, by your peers, your teachers, your boss, by society. You have bought into the lie that you need to be a certain way, or achieve certain things, in order to be loved. When you make a mistake, you judge yourself and make it into a big problem. Your mind goes over it time and time again "how could I be so stupid?" When a child makes a mistake, it laughs about it and then goes on playing. They totally forgets about it. Try to imagine a one year old telling himself: *"Oh no, I fell over again when I tried to get that cookie from the dinner table, it's terrible! How can I be so stupid?"* It sounds ridiculous doesn't it? But in a way this is what we are doing to ourselves all the time.

You are judging yourself because you don't love yourself. If you totally loved yourself, there would be no need to judge yourself any longer. So you can say that love is the absence of judgement.

Love is the absence of Fear

When you say you love someone, there is the desire to own, to possess that person: "Now you are mine", "You are my baby." We don't want to lose this person, we want to to possess him or her. Possessiveness is based on fear. We call this love, but we don't know a love without fear, without possession.

When you realise this, the only logical conclusion is that a marriage can never be based on love. It is the ultimate form of "holding on", of possessing the other person. "Now she is my wife, she is exclusively mine, and we will stay together for the rest of our lives"...

We read and talk about "true love", "divine love", a pure love of the heart. The only way we can experience real love is when we can let go of the fear, the possessiveness. As Krishnamurti says: *"as long as we possess we shall not love."* All this fear, the jealousy and possession is a process of the mind. Only when the mind is quiet is there love. Only then can your heart be pure, unpolluted by the mind.

Love is freedom

When you let go of jealousy, of possessiveness, of fear then you will feel what real love is: freedom. Most of the time when you love somebody there is a need behind that love, it gives you something, the love from this person is filling a hole inside of you. "*I love you so much*" you say to the other person, but when they decide to end the relationship and withdraw their love, then suddenly you hate that person.

Only when you become whole yourself, when you totally love yourself, can you love the other person without any need behind it. Now you can truly love that person, just for how they are, without a need to get something from them. If you truly love the other person you will want them to be happy. So that means that if they want to go to a football match with some friends you let them go, because you want them to be happy. The holding on, the possessiveness stops. Why would you ever limit the person who you love? Instead, you set them free with your love. Just like in that song from Sting: "*If you love somebody, set them free.*" And when you are free, there is no need to escape, to run away. You will want to come back to this freedom.

There is no limit to love

The magical thing about love is that it has no limit. It is not that you only have a finite amount of love that you can give to people. Love is unlimited, in fact the more you give it, the more love you will feel yourself.

The more you love yourself, the more you will feel love for other people. When you become like a Buddha, you will feel love for all sentient beings. You will experience a love without any needs behind it. When you are whole you don't need anything from the other person in order to make you feel better, to fill a hole inside you.

It is perfectly natural to love more than one person. There is no limit to love. You can experience this with your children: you can love each one as much as the other. When you get a second child it does not mean that you love the first one less. There is no limit to your love for your children. The same can happen with other people. A man can love several women at the same time, or a woman can love several men at the same time. There is nothing abnormal about this, only in our society this is usually not accepted. If a man tells his partner that he feels real love for another woman it probably causes a major problem in the relationship. You can love all of our children, you can love all of your friends and family, but when you love another person of the opposite sex it is not ok. It just doesn't make sense when you think about it.

I have experienced this myself, especially after my awakening experience. I can feel love for several women at the same time, but it doesn't mean that I engage in a (sexual) relationship with them.

Now some people who read about these kind of concepts take this as the validation to just go off and have sex with different people. That is not love, that is just selfish. To love several people at once is at best confusing, and it can lead to a total disaster if you are not free of attachments and needs. To act out on these feelings and engage in a form of (sexual) relationship can cause a lot of suffering, for the others and for yourself. That is why I see most people who experiment with polygamy end with painful breakups and lots of suffering. It can only work if all people involved are free of needs, when they totally love themselves. And that is very rare.

50
Love or Fear

> *"Love is what we were born with,*
> *Fear is what we learned here"*
> Marianne Williamson

When you break it down, everything comes down to just one choice: love or fear. Every thought you have, every action you take, every decision you make: are you acting out of love, or out of fear? Another way to put it is this: do you follow your mind or your heart? Your mind is always based on fear, your heart is love.

Especially when you need to make important decisions, we often get told to be "sensible" and make a rational choice. Many of us choose an education or career based on rational thinking: "with this qualification I can get a good job and earn a decent income", rather than follow their heart, their passion.

If there is one message that is always consistent from the guides it is this: learn to follow your heart and act out of love. If there was only one message that you could take away from this book, then please remember this. If you really apply this principle it will totally transform your life.

Sometimes it is easy to see what you would do if you chose love, sometimes it is harder to see.

- The woman who gets beaten by her husband. Does she stay out of love or out of fear?
- Do I chose to study dance, my passion, or law, like my father is suggesting? What would your heart choose?
- Your marriage is in a very difficult phase. Then you fall in love with another man. Do you act on it? Do you tell your husband? What would love do?
- You don't really love your husband anymore, but he provides for you and your two children. If you leave, the children don't get to

see their father every day. Do you stay or do you leave him? What does love choose here?

Sometimes it will take some time to figure out what the most loving choice is, and you need to look and feel deeply into each option to determine if this is based on love or fear. Often we are so cut off from our heart, so much in our mind, that it is hard to see which is which. Like anything, the more you practice, the easier it gets in time. The more you connect to your heart, the more you will hear its call.

Sometimes there are moments when you know that your next decision will completely change the course of your life. I have had this experience, here is that story:

When I was living in Holland my life was sorted. I had a small but beautiful house next to a canal in nature just outside of town, I had a job that I loved with an enormous amount of freedom, the company even paid for my aura reading studies! I had a company car, great income, good pension, lots of friends.

One weekend I was going to visit my friend Michael in London. The night before I was watching TV and drifted off a bit. I got a daydream that "tomorrow I will meet a woman, she is blonde, pretty and very spiritual, and we will have a relationship together." Then I got back to my senses. "What? That's a crazy fantasy" I thought and I totally forgot about it.

The next day I flew to London, and when I got to Michael's house he told me that his father had got tickets to see the opera "Madame Butterfly" at the Royal Albert Hall. They had invited some friends, did I mind? I said "of course not", and that afternoon people arrived at his house so we could all go together. At one point Leona walked into the room. The moment she walked in a jolt of energy ran through my body. That was her - this was the woman of my vision! She was blonde and very beautiful. I didn't know what to do, but when we got introduced she said "Oh you are Stef! Michael's dad told me that you write with the guides, can I sit next to you? I want to hear all about it." Of course I agreed.

Six months later we were in deeply in love, but there was a slight problem: she lived in England and was about to start her psychology studies and I lived in Holland. She was made redundant and came to stay with me for a month. It was great and we both knew that we wanted to be together. She could not see herself moving to Holland. She had come from The Czech Republic to England ten years before and had to build up her life. She could not imagine doing it all over again and having to learn to speak Dutch on top of it. How would she ever manage to be a psychotherapist in Holland? "You speak a very good English, why don't you come to England instead?" she said.

It was crunch time. I knew that I had to make a decision, and I knew that it would completely change the course of my life. Quite literally this was a choice between my heart (Leona) and the sensible choice (keep my secure life, everything that I had built up in Holland). When I thought about the choice, it became clear that what would keep me in Holland was fear. Fear for the unknown, fear to lose what I had: the house that I totally renovated myself and that I loved, fear to give up my job, my friends. But I knew that if I let Leona go, I would regret it for the rest of my life. So in the end I decided to choose love, not fear. Within two months I had sold my house, left my job and moved to England.

Now I am not going to say that it was easy, or that this is a tale of happy ever after. Being in England was much harder than I ever imagined. After being together for eleven years, Leona and I separated. Leona was drawn back to The Czech Republic and was spending more and more time there. I stayed in England with our daughter. I have made many mistakes in my life, and I have made many mistakes during our marriage, but the decision to leave Holland and be with Leona in England has been one of the best decisions of my life. I have no regrets. She remains one of the closest people in my life and we work together in The Czech Republic these days.

51
The Illusion of Happiness

"If you want to be happy, be"
Leo Tolstoy

We are living in a society where we are constantly being fed the message that we need to get something, to achieve something, in order to be happy. You need to get a good job, have enough money in the bank account, find a partner, get married, buy a nice house, have two children, go on a nice holiday once or preferably twice a year. Then you will be happy.

All marketing and sales is based on this: If you buy this new BMW your status will go up and you will be happier. Want to look and feel great? You need Ray-ban sunglasses and this Prada bag. Oh, and what about a new hairstyle? All adverts show young and beautiful people, always in the sunshine, preferably on a beach or some other beautiful location. Just buy this product and you will feel this good too...

Does it work? Are you happy? How long does that feeling of happiness in your new BMW last, before that too becomes normal? We save up all year to have a two week long dream holiday. Then after one week back at work we are as stressed and miserable as before, having to wait a whole year before we can go on holiday again.

We tell ourselves a story; that if we just reach the goals that we set for ourselves, then we will be happy. But the problem is that by the time you have reached your goal, you will have formulated a new one. You have seen an even better house. Just when you finally bought that BMW, a new model is coming out that is even better. And so you start chasing this new goal.

Even the majority of people who are consciously on a "spiritual path" join in this madness. The spiritual version of this is *"The*

Secret", the "Law of Attraction." We are told that if we just think positive and believe that there is an abundance, we will be able to attract this abundance in our lives. In the movie, people who have "made it" are telling you that you too can be super successful. So millions of people buy the book and watch the movie. It is still the same message but now wrapped in a layer of spirituality: buy this book, buy this DVD and we will show you how you can become successful and rich. Then you will be happy.

One of the most successful and richest, pop artist of all time was Michael Jackson. Did he seem very happy to you? You can find many, many examples like this: Elvis, Marilyn Monroe, Kurt Cobain... Despite their success, despite their wealth, they were not happy. Or maybe paradoxically, it was because of their success. As long as you have not made it to the top, you can still believe in the illusion, you still have something to strive for. But then one day you reach the top. Now what? You have reached the top and still you are not happy. And it can only go downhill from there... This realisation can create such suffering, that sometimes it leads to suicide.

What do you need to be happy? Did Buddha have the latest iPhone? Wireless internet? One million followers on Instagram? 1000 likes on his latest Facebook post? The latest BMW? Or even better, a Tesla Model S? Did he get a promotion? A certificate to put on the wall for achieving buddhahood?

We make the mistake that we always compare ourselves with someone else. He has a bigger house, a better car, earns more money, his partner is younger and more beautiful. You want to be in his shoes, in his position, you want to have what they have. In England there is an expression for this: "keeping up with the Jones's."

But here is the thing. When you are reading this book, you are one of the people who are living a lifestyle that only 1 billion people on the planet can afford. This means that there are six billion people in the world who would do anything to have what you have. They believe that if they had what you have now, they would be totally happy...

Here is the good news:
You don't need to get anything in order to be happy.
You don't need to achieve anything in order to be happy.
You don't need to do anything in order to be happy.
In order to be happy, you need to let go.

To let go of your fears.
To let go of your attachments.
To let go of your desires.

In order to be happy you just need to be.
To be loving, to love yourself, to be yourself.
There is nothing to do, nothing to reach.

52
Letting go

"Don't cling to a mistake just because you spent a long time making it"
Aubrey De Grey

"Attachment is the root of all suffering"
Buddha

One of the fundamental truths that the Buddha taught is this: *"Nothing is permanent but change."*
You can observe this in nature: trees will blossom and grow new fresh leaves in spring, have full green foliage in summer, turn to yellow and golden in autumn, until the winds will blow the last leaf away. In winter the tree is barren, resting, gathering strength for spring. It is a continuous movement of change.

Can you imagine if there was a tree that was desperately trying to hold on to its leaves? You would laugh at it, telling it that it is pointless, that it is part of nature to lose your leaves in autumn. But this is exactly what we humans do. Children are still in touch with nature, they are used to change all the time, they don't resist it. But the older we get, the more we want things to remain the same. We need to learn from nature. A forest in autumn shows you just how beautiful letting go can be.

In this society we get taught to hold on, to cling to everything. The more things you can gather and hold on to, the more successful you are supposed to be. You hold on your title, your job, your profession, your status, your money, your possessions. You cling to your memories, your photos. You hold on to your body, your youth. You hold on to your friends, your family, your pet, your partner, your husband or wife. Marriage is the ultimate festival of holding on. There is only one thing that we hold on to even more: our children.

How much time and energy do you spend in your life trying to hold on to things or people? How free would you be if you could learn to just let go? There is a beautiful Native American saying: *"When a horse is dead, get off"*

Holding on is based on fear. Letting go is love.

Let this sink in for a moment. Read it again. Holding on is based on fear, letting go is based on love. Think for yourself – is this true? Once you "get it" it will create a huge shift inside of you.

One of the keys to happiness is to learn to let go. In letting go you stop resisting, you stop wasting your energy, you align with the flow of life. Letting go creates space, and that space holds a tremendous energy, an opening to new experiences, an opening to experience more love in your life. Letting go is part of Emptiness, and Emptiness leads to Bliss.

Let go of your attachments,
Let go of your fears,
Let go of your desires,
And you will experience freedom,
You will experience love.

53
Death

"I'm not afraid of death, I just don't want to be there when it happens"
Woody Allen

"Everybody dies – but not everybody lives"
Prince Ea

The ultimate act of letting go is to let go of your own life, to die. In order to be totally free of fear, you will also need to let go of your fear of dying. Most people are afraid of death. We pretend it won't happen. As if just by not thinking about it, it will not happen. But guess what? We are all going to die. Your grandparents will die. Your parents will die. Your friends will die. Your partner will die. Your child will die. You will die.

What do you feel now, as you are reading this? Is it uncomfortable to be confronted with this? So what do you do, do you go into fear? Into resistance? Or can you accept something that is inevitable? When you look at it, really think about it, then the only sane thing to do is to accept it. It is not like you have any other choice. And this acceptance will set you free. Only from this acceptance can you get to a place of peace.

Here is another uncomfortable truth: nobody knows when they are going to die. We build a story in our mind, that because we are living a healthy lifestyle and we get good medical care, we should live to at least 80 years old, maybe even 90 or 100. But you might die tomorrow. You might go to sleep tonight and never wake up again. You might have a car crash, a heart attack, anything could happen. This might be your last day on earth.

There is a very profound Zen practise: "Dying every day." Every night before you go to sleep, think back on your day. How was your day? What are you grateful for? Then realise that this could be your last day on earth. Make peace with whatever you need to make peace with, then say goodbye to the world. When you wake up in the morning, realise that you have been given another day here on earth. This could be your last day on earth. This is an amazing gift, and you may feel a smile coming on your face, a joy in your heart. Be grateful, and set your intentions for the day.

It is such an amazing way to start the day. When you practice the art of dying every day, every day becomes precious, becomes a special day. You will be more in the now.

Dying before you die

Let's take this practice one step further. Can you die right now? Not in 50 years or so, but today? When you die your brain dies, it stops working. The whole process of remembering and thinking stops. Death is the end of thoughts.

Can you die to all of your attachments, worries, fears, hopes, so completely that you wake up completely fresh, young, vital? The only way to be completely fresh, is to completely let go of the past.

But we hold on to the past, because we *are* the past. All our thoughts are based on the past, all our knowledge is based on the past. Your whole identity is based on the past: it is based on all your experiences, all your memories, all your thoughts. All that is based on the past.

Can you die to everything that you know? What happens when you let go of all that? Then you end your past. The mind can be aware of the unknown only when it dies to the known. Only when the mind dies to the known can it find out what death is while you are living. In that very discovery is freedom from fear.

Letting go of thought is letting go of fear. Fear is always created by thought. I am afraid that the pain that happened yesterday might happen again tomorrow. It is these thoughts that create the fear. Therefore to end fear you need to end your thoughts. Can you just observe the situation and not start a thought process about it? This is the way to stop your thinking.

The fear when there is a bus coming at you and you need to move out of the way, is not the fear that I am talking about here. That is a natural self-protecting intelligence, saying: "you need to get out of the way of this bus NOW!" But all the other fears that you have are created by your thoughts. Can you die before you are dying? Can you die today?

Only when there is a dying to the past, then there is love. When you let go of all thoughts, you also let go of all fears, because fear is created by thoughts. And the absence of fear is love. Love is not memory, love is not pleasure. Only when you die to the past, die to all the conflict, all the sorrow, all the fear, then there is love. Then you are free. Then you can do what you will.

Love is only possible when there is death. Only when you die to the past are you truly living. There is no separation between living and dying. In that very ending there is renewal, newness, freshness, innocence. Only when your die to the past can there be a true love. Death and Life and Love are one and the same.

54
Nothing really matters

"If it is not important at death, then it is not important now"
Unknown

We spend most of our time worrying about things that will either work themselves out anyway, or that don't really matter in the long run.

Think of the problem that you have today. Will it matter in a week from now? In six months time? In two years? When you look at the issues in your life in this way, you will quickly see that they are not as important as your mind wants to make them.

"Where do I find vegan cakes for the party tomorrow?"
A week from now this will not be an issue anymore.
"Should my daughter go to this school or the other one?"
In a few months time this will no longer trouble your mind.
"Planning permission for the new house I want to build was refused, but this house is falling apart, what do I do now?"
In a few years time, all this will have been resolved one way or another.
"My partner is leaving me, how can I go on with my life without her?"
In a couple of years you will look back and see that life did move on, and find that you have grown enormously.

Most of the time when you think back about the problems you had a few months ago, you laugh about it. When you consider how much mental energy you spent on it, you can see how ridiculous it was and you will laugh. So if you will be laughing about your problem in six months time, then why not laugh about it now?

When you start putting this into practice you are starting to train your mind to let go of its grip on you. It doesn't mean that you will just let everything happen to you, you will still take action and do your bit, but it will not affect you so much, you will not be so attached to a particular outcome. Your stress levels will reduce dramatically.

When you really look at things, you will find that nothing really matters. When you are about to die and look back at your current situation, does it really matter?
Your holiday in Spain – does it matter?
Whether your friend can meet up tomorrow or not – does it matter?
That amazing meal in the five star restaurant – does it matter?
Whether this person wants to have sex with you tonight or not – does it matter?
Whether you get that promotion or not – does it matter?
Your country wins the world cup football – does it matter?
Whether you meet the deadline for this important project at work or not – does it matter?
Your country hosts the Olympic games – does it matter?
England decides to leave the EU – does it matter?
Whether you build a new house, or renovate the old one, or move to another one – does it matter?
Being sick in bed with flu – does it matter?
Backpacking around Asia for six months – does it matter?
Whether you get that business contract or not – does it matter?
Whether this book sells a hundred copies or hundred thousand – does it matter?

Probably with some of the things I listed here you will have felt a resistance coming up. Good! I invite you to really look into this. Meditate on it and find out for yourself: does it really matter or not?

When you are about to die, you will find that none of this matters any more. Nobody is going to stand up at your funeral and say: "she had such great shoes and such a beautiful house." Material success doesn't matter at all. You arrive on the earth with nothing and you will leave the earth with nothing. You can't take anything with you.

There is only one thing that you take with you when you die: your soul. So what matters are the matters of your soul. Did you live?

Did you grow? Did you love? Did you say to your loved ones what you wanted to say? Are you at peace with yourself? Did your soul heal? Did your soul grow? Ultimately that is the only thing that matters in life.

> **Exercise:**
>
> If you knew that you would die in your sleep tonight, would you be at peace? Are there people that you still need to say things to?

55
Who am I?

*"The desire to know your own soul will end
all other desires"*
Rumi

Who am I? You may have asked yourself this question sometimes, and it is not so easy to answer it. You started to form an idea of yourself from when you were about one year old. You started to realise that you have a name, that you have a mummy and daddy. You are a boy or a girl. You start to realise that this is my body, my house, my toys. From then on you have been collecting more and more ideas about yourself during all of your life. Let us examine these thoughts.

Are you your body? You might think that you are, because you might be a girl for example, with brown hair and brown eyes. But what happens if you lose both your legs. Are you still you? Of course you are, but you might change your identity a bit. Now you are a disabled person. But the real *you* remains the same. The same person is inside this body, looking out of these eyes, looking at the world. You have a body, but you are not your body.

Are you your emotions? You will experience emotions, you will feel happy or sad, or depressed. Sometimes you are completely taken over by your emotions, sometimes for very long periods of time. You might say: "I am depressed." But emotions come and go. Even that depression will lift one day. You have your emotions, but *you* are not your emotions.

What about your thoughts, are you your thoughts? Our identification with our thoughts is so strong that our whole experience of life is determined by the thoughts that we have inside our head. One day you might be walking on a beach on a sunny day and feel fantastic. You have a new special person in your life, you are in love. Summer is on its way, and everything seems to be working out finally. On another day you are walking on a beach on a sunny day and you feel terrible. You feel alone, nobody was available to meet up with at the weekend. Once again you did not get the job that you went to interview for. Autumn is on its way and the days are getting shorter. Your life is in a rut.

It is the same beach, the same sunny day. The only thing that is different are the thoughts inside your head. Imagine that you could stop your thoughts and just experience the actual moment, you would feel the warmth of the sun on your skin, see the sunshine sparkling on the water. The experience of both days would be exactly the same. So what is real? The "normal" version of that day, or the one with no thoughts? The whole problem is that our normal version, the one with our thoughts, feels so damn real.

Are you your thoughts? Most people identify themselves completely with the thoughts they have created about themselves. For example, I might say that I am Stef, that I am a man, that I am Dutch but live in England, that I am divorced, that I am a father, that I am a healer, that I am a spiritual teacher, that I am a writer, that I am optimistic, that I am this and that. All these identifications are descriptions of the person "Stef Kling" that I have formed in my mind. It is the story that I have formed about me. Your personality is nothing but a constantly repeated thought construction. You have constructed a mental map full of stories about your personality, about yourself, and you believe it to be true.

We all do this, and we are so mind-identified that we think that this is who we are. But what if I had a car accident and could not work as a healer anymore? What if my daughter died in that same accident, then I also wouldn't be a father anymore. Who am I then? Am I still me? Who am I? Who is asking these questions? When I am observing my thoughts, who is observing?

I was discussing all this with my daughter Vicky one day (she was only 13 years old) and she said: "Well of course I am not my body, and my brain is part of my body, and my thoughts come from my brain. So that means that I cannot be my thoughts." It was a perfect logic. So if you are not your thoughts, then who are you?

The second person in your head

Have you ever had the realisation that although you have got older and have had different experiences in life, *you* have remained the same? I have always had this feeling very strongly. Now, as I am writing this book, I am 48 years old, but I am essentially the same as when I was 33 and came to England, or when I was 19 and competing for a place in the Dutch Around The World sailing team. Yes, my body has aged, I have had a lot of different experiences, but *I* am the same. Who am I?

There is actually a second being inside of you. The first one is the one we normally identify ourselves with: our mind, our thoughts. But there is a second being: the observer. This is the aspect of you that is watching you go through life. This is the part of you that loves you unconditionally. This is the part of you that does not die when your body dies. This is the part of you that feels the same whether you are 19, 33 or 48 years old. This is your soul, your Self. When you realise this, it is literally a realisation of the Self, Self-realisation.

Everything that you have thought of yourself so far is not real. It is fiction, it has got nothing to do with you. All of your goals, your worries, your fears, your hopes, they are all imagined. It is all a construction of your mind. It is all an illusion. That is not who you are. You are the observer, the timeless, the Self. You, the Self, don't have to do anything, you don't need to achieve anything. Your real being is profound peace, eternal stillness, total purity, infinite love, pure light. You are life itself.

Exercise

Find a partner to work with you. Sit opposite each other, and look at each other. Then one person will ask: "Who are you?" Don't think too much about the answer, just say the first thing that comes into your mind. Then the other person asks again: "Who are you?" Repeat this over and over, until no more answers come.

It might go something like this:

"Who are you?"
I am Stef Kling.
"Who are you?"
I am Dutch.
 "Who are you?"
I am a father.
"Who are you?"
 I am a divorced.
"Who are you?"
I am a healer.
"Who are you?"
 I am a writer.
Etc, etc...

See what happens. Sometimes by continuously asking this question, you will go beyond the personality, beyond the mind, and get a glimpse of your real self.

56
Why am I here?

> *"We are not humans having a spiritual experience,*
> *we are spirit having a human experience"*
> Pierre Teilhard de Chardin

> *"The Soul is expressing itself through the I"*
> Roberto Assagioli

Why am I here? What is the purpose of my life? This question can only be answered by looking at the bigger picture, not from the perspective of your ego, your limited mind.

This is not the first time that you are here on earth. You have been here many times before, and you will likely come back again many times after you leave your body behind.

You are eternal spirit, having an experience of being human on this amazing and beautiful planet that we call Earth.

When we arrive here, when we are born, we forget our true nature and we fall into a collective trance, we get absorbed by the collective consciousness that is here on earth at this time in history. We get domesticated, we get trained how to be a "good human", according to the norms and values of society at this moment in time. Then when our "training" is complete, when we become an adult, we set out to create a life for our self. At some point we wake up spiritually and embark on a journey to understand life. This is when the question arises: what is the purpose of my life?

For many years I have been doing readings for people, where I write with their spirit guides. Every time people ask the question: "why am I here, what is the purpose of my life?" The answer is essentially the same, and it is made up of two things:

- Firstly to heal yourself and to grow
- Secondly to share your gift with the world.

We are here to heal our life, to heal our wounds. We all got wounded in love. And we carry within us the wounds of past lives. We are here to heal that too. We are here to grow, to raise our consciousness. To step into our power, to let go of fear, to return to love. You are here to remember who you really are, to return to your true nature, your pure state. All the rest is irrelevant.

And you have a gift to share with the world. You are totally unique. There is nobody on this planet who is like you, who brings a certain energy, certain qualities like you have. Without you, the world would not be the same. If you were not here, many people would miss you, they would miss your energy, your love, your light, your whole being.

In Psychosynthesis there is a beautiful saying:

> *"The soul is expressing itself through the I"*

What that means is that when you are born, your soul decides to express itself here on the earth. In order to do that it needs a body, and a personality, an ego, an "I." When your personality and your soul are aligned, your soul can really express itself on earth. When you have healed your wounds, when you have let go of fear and self judgment, you can express yourself freely. You can work with inspiration, choose freely to follow it or not, making choices and living completely from a place of love. You will be shining your light, whatever it is that you decide to do. You whole being will light up the world and you will ignite the light in others. By giving yourself permission to be totally yourself you will give others the permission to do the same. That is what your life is about. Or like Ram Dass put it: *"we are here to guide each other home."*

Your soul does not want you to be stuck in the same job that you have been doing for the last ten years and that you don't enjoy.
Your soul wants to have experiences.
Your soul wants to heal,

Your soul wants to grow.
Your soul wants to be free, to play.
Your soul wants to experience life, totally and completely.
Your soul wants to feel: both pain and pleasure, both fear and love, so that it can learn to let go of fear and choose love.
Your soul wants to bring love and beauty into the world,
To illuminate the world,
To enlighten the world.

> *"If you want to awaken all of humanity, then awaken all of yourself. If you want to eliminate all of suffering in the world, then illuminate all that is dark and negative in yourself. Truly, the greatest gift you have to give is that of your own self-transformation"*
> Lao Tzu

57
You are already enlightened

Recently I asked my guides what I need to do to get into a permanent state of enlightenment. Do I need to find a teacher? A guru who will help me make the final jump? They said: "No, you will do this by yourself", then they wrote this:

Just allow yourself to be totally yourself
Let go of all your fears
Give yourself permission to be Buddha
Have no agenda
Allow the energy to flow through you
Allow the joy to flow through you
Just do what you love doing

It sounds so simple, yet it's so hard to do. Or is it?

A few weeks later I discovered the work of the American Zen master Dennis Genpo Merzel. In his workshops he invites people to speak from the enlightened aspect within themselves, something that he calls "Big Mind", and people change right in front of his eyes. He says: "You need permission to be enlightened. Permission is the key. Everybody has this enlightened aspect already inside them. In fact, everybody is enlightened already, only nobody gets invited to live from this enlightened state." His method is described in his brilliant book "*Big Mind - Big Heart.*"

"You are already enlightened", you hear this a lot these days. But just because a lot of people are repeating a message does not mean that it is true. The core message from Advaita (non-duality) teachers like Papaji and Mooji is that you are already perfect; you are already enlightened, only you don't realise it. Once you completely recognise this, when you awaken, you will become enlightened. I partly agree with this, but also I don't. Let me explain.

It is true that in our core we are perfect, we are whole. Our core is pure spirit, pure light, pure love. But we developed an ego, a mind-identity, and we got wounded in this life. All this is keeping us away from mental peace.

In Part One, I defined enlightenment in its simplest form as "a state of permanent mental peace." How many people do you know that are in a state of permanent mental peace? Just because someone had an awakening experience does not mean they are enlightened. Yes, the potential is there in all of us, but to attain a state of permanent peace is not so easy to do. Only a handful of people have arrived at this place.

But... there is one development that gives me great hope. In the past only a small group of people had access to spiritual teachings. This was mostly done orally, in monasteries, churches, mosques or ashrams. And only a few chosen ones got access to the full teachings.

These days, with the advance of the internet and the flow of information that followed, teachings that were previously only available for the initiates are now available for anyone. Sacred Buddhist and Yogic teachings are now out in the open. Something like Reiki, once a secret healing method, is now considered a "basic" healing tool. Ironically the occupation of Tibet by China has resulted in the spreading of Tibetan Buddhism worldwide.

Millions of people are now on a conscious spiritual journey, combining this with a "normal" life. Yoga, meditation and more recently mindfulness, have become mainstream practices. For example, a recent survey found that in Holland one third of the adult population is doing a regular practice of yoga, meditation or mindfulness. More people follow a vegetarian or vegan diet. There is a huge surge of awareness around food and natural health. All this is causing a huge shift in consciousness and this will continue to have a ripple effect. At some point, these trends will reach a critical mass, a tipping point, and penetrate all of society. I believe that we will see a total transformation of human consciousness, and as a result the way we live will be transformed in the next 20 years.

58
Life without limits

The only limits in your life are the limits in your mind. I am not talking here about getting a better job with more income, finding a new partner or anything like that. I am talking about a whole new fundamental way of living.

When I had my awakening experience I just *knew* that we don't have to die when we get 100 years old. We can live way beyond that, whilst remaining perfectly healthy and functional. Here is a list of things that humans can achieve to stretch your thinking of what is possible. All of this has been done already:

You can live on light, on Prana, without any eating any food.
You can live to be 200 years old, in perfect health.
You can move an object just with your mind.
You can manifest an object out of thin air.
You can appear in two places at the same time.
You can keep yourself warm outside in the snow with a temperature of -20°C without wearing any clothes.
You can leave your body, explore the astral plane and come back into your body again.

You are eternal spirit in a human body. You create your own reality. The only limitation is the limitation in your mind. You are not your mind. Once you truly realise this, you will realise that anything is possible.

What do you choose to do with your life?

59
Total Freedom

A friend of mine wrote the following one day:

"Yesterday when I was listening to some tracks from the early 90's I was transported back in time... Back to the "real" me, the girl I know so deeply, but had lost along the way. The girl who was comfortable in her own skin, who laughed and loved, all the time, who was full of light, who lifted every soul she met on the way, the one who danced and sung and smiled and was unquestionably happy, for no reason whatsoever, other than that she was alive. The one who had not been hurt, betrayed, and traumatised by pain and fear. I'd forgotten about that girl, until I heard the music. Forgotten what it was like to be truly happy, to be truly me. And I want to find her again. I want to be her again. I want her back. But, how?"

What she described so beautifully is a universal desire. The desire to return to the pureness, the innocence, the freedom of our childhood. It is the desire to return to our true nature, which is love.

And it is possible. It is totally possible to return to this state of love, of freedom, of wholeness. This book describes the path to this place: Emptiness and Bliss. You need to become empty again: to heal the wounds, to release the pain and fear that is stored inside you, to let go of limiting beliefs. You need to return to Bliss: to raise your frequency, to heal your body, to build a healthy ego, so that you can then reduce the ego, to raise your consciousness, to let go of fear, to let go of judgment, to love yourself again, totally and unconditionally.

And bit by bit you will fall in love again, not with a man or woman, but with life. Until in the end you are totally intoxicated with the beauty that is all around you. You will feel the wonder of life, just like you did as a child. Everything will be fresh, everything will feel brighter, more alive somehow. You will have arrived home again. Home in yourself.

This is the most important journey that you can take in your life. In a way this is more important than enlightenment. You might not be totally free of suffering, you will still experience pain, but you will find that you will shift out of this state very quickly and return to love again. It doesn't matter if you experience full enlightenment or not, because you will be free.

When you are free of fear, when you are free of the pain of your past, you will be free to express yourself in this world in any way that you want. You will shine your light and you will light up others along the way.

60
Permanent peace

"Don't rest in peace, live in peace"
Unknown

Permanent peace comes from inside of you

Let go of your judgements

Let go of your fears

Let go of the past

Forgive others

Forgive yourself

Accept yourself how you are

Stop worrying about the future

Be totally present in the moment

Realise that nothing is permanent but change

Allow life to flow and unfold itself

Remember that you know nothing

Listen to inspiration

Live your life out of love, not fear

Become empty

Enter into bliss

Give yourself permission to shine

Shine your light into the world

Epilogue

I hope that this book has given you a better understanding of the concepts of Emptiness and Bliss, and the benefits of combining Energy with Consciousness. The more empty you become, the more space there is for the bliss to come in. I hope that the five principles will serve as a useful guide to apply this into your life:

1. Raise your frequency = bliss
2. Release your emotions = emptiness
3. Heal your ego = emptiness and bliss
4. Raise your consciousness = emptiness and bliss
5. Connect to source = bliss

The path to enlightenment that I have outlined in this book can be seen as a synthesis between the traditional Buddhist and Yoga paths and modern New Age spirituality. It connects the teachings from the masters that I have discussed in this book. Krishnamurti, Adyashanti and Mooji focus completely on consciousness and meditation. Eckhart Tolle was on the right path with his concept of the pain body, only his method to "focus on the now" has its limitations. Osho perhaps came closest to this synthesis; he encouraged people to go into therapy and release emotions through Dynamic Meditation.

I explained that it doesn't matter if you become awakened or fully enlightened. It is perhaps better to be in an awakened state, with a small ego that enables you to function in the world. What matters is that you are free, that you let go of fear, of judgment. That you have mental peace. That you come into a state of love and live out of love. That you share your gift with the world.

I hope that this book will help you on your journey. If you would like to work with me personally, or want to attend one of my talks or workshops, you can find information on: www.stefkling.com.

With love,
Stef Kling

Printed in Great Britain
by Amazon